DBT SKILLS FOR MENTAL HEALTH

A NEURODIVERGENT FRIENDLY GUIDE FOR TEENS ON MANAGING SOCIAL ANXIETY, STRESS, DEPRESSION, ANGER, AND ADHD WITH POSITIVE PSYCHOLOGY FOR EMOTIONAL REGULATION

DON BARLOW

A ROADTOTRANQUILITY(™) BOOK

© Copyright 2023 - **All rights reserved.**

The content contained within this book may not be reproduced, duplicated, or transmitted without direct written permission from the author or the publisher.

Under no circumstances will any blame or legal responsibility be held against the publisher, or author, for any damages, reparation, or monetary loss due to the information contained within this book, either directly or indirectly.

Legal Notice:

This book is copyright protected. It is only for personal use. You cannot amend, distribute, sell, use, quote, or paraphrase any part, or the content within this book, without the author or publisher's permission.

Disclaimer Notice:

Please note that the information contained within this document is for educational and entertainment purposes only. All effort has been executed to present accurate, up-to-date, reliable, complete information. No warranties of any kind are declared or implied. Readers acknowledge that the author is not rendering legal, financial, medical, or professional advice. The content within this book has been derived from various sources. Please consult a licensed professional before attempting any techniques outlined in this book.

By reading this document, the reader agrees that under no circumstances is the author responsible for any losses, direct or indirect, that are incurred due to the use of the information in this document, including, but not limited to, errors, omissions, or inaccuracies.

CONTENTS

Introduction   7

Part I
MENTAL HEALTH ISSUES AND DBT

1. **WHAT ABOUT MY MENTAL HEALTH?**   17
   - Mental Health; What's the Fuss all About?   18
   - Adolescent Years   22
   - Risk Factors for Mental Illness Conditions   23
   - Debunking Mental Health Myths   26
   - Maintaining Your Mental Health   27

2. **NEURODIVERGENCE EXPLAINED AND THE ROLE OF DBT IN MENTAL HEALTH**   29
   - Neurodiversity: What it is and What it isn't   29
   - Common Neurodivergent Myth Busters   30
   - Neurodivergent Conditions   33
   - Neurodivergents, What Makes Them Tick?   34
   - Why is a diagnosis of Neurodivergent Important?   34
   - Empowerment versus Weakness   36

3. **DBT (DIALECTICAL BEHAVIORAL THERAPY)**   39
   - The Four Major Components of DBT   40
   - The Role of DBT in Mental Health   43

4. **MINDFULNESS**   45
   - What does Being in the Present Mean?   46
   - The Benefits of Mindfulness   49

5. **EMOTIONAL REGULATION**   53
   - Bad and Good Emotions   54
   - Feelings are just feelings   56

How do You Identify your Feelings?	61
Self-Talk	67
6. INTERPERSONAL EFFECTIVENESS	**71**
What Are Your Challenges with Your Communication Now?	72
How you express yourself is a form of communication	75
How to Improve Your Interpersonal Skills	78
7. DISTRESS TOLERANCE	**91**
Survival	92
Self-soothing	96
What Are Your Emotions Telling You?	98

Part II
COMPREHENSIVE DBT APPROACH: SOCIAL ANXIETY, STRESS MANAGEMENT, AND DEPRESSION

8. MANAGING SOCIAL ANXIETY IN NEURODIVERGENTS	**105**
Symptoms of Social Anxiety	106
Managing Social Anxiety Using DBT Principles	114
DBT Rain Technique	117
9. MANAGING STRESS IN NEURODIVERGENTS	**119**
Stress in Neurodivergents	121
Guided Mindfulness Techniques for Relaxation	123
Time Management Tips for a Stress-Free Day	127
10. MANAGING DEPRESSION IN NEURODIVERGENTS	**137**
What is Depression?	138
Common Causes of Depression	139
Tips for Managing and Preventing Depression	142
Tips for Managing Depression	143

Part III
COMPREHENSIVE DBT APPROACH: ANGER, ADHD

11. MANAGING ANGER IN NEURODIVERGENTS 157
    DBT Techniques for Anger 162
    Anger Management Skills for Divergents 169

12. MANAGING ADHD IN NEURODIVERGENTS 175
    What is ADHD? 175
    Using DBT Principles to Manage ADHD 181
    What Are Your Super-Powers? 190

13. OVERVIEW: EVERYTHING YOU NEED TO KNOW TO KEEP A HEALTHY MIND AND BODY 197
    Top 10 Tips for Living a Mindful and More Emotionally Stable Life 198

Conclusion 205
Useful Information Section and Further Tools 213
Resources 215
Notes 221

Before we get into the book, let me offer you a free mini-book. **Scan this QR code** to claim your FREE *People-Pleasing No More* mini-book!

INTRODUCTION

Be yourself, everyone else is taken

— OSCAR WILDE

I love this quote from Oscar Wilde as it sums up that we are all different. Being authentic and ourselves isn't that easy for all of us, especially if you have been diagnosed with a neurodivergent condition. The word 'neurodivergent' means that your brain works differently than the 'normal' brain, whatever normal means. You may find that you simply behave, think, and learn differently, which is all the word 'neurodivergent' means. I will break this down in a later chapter and give you more information, but at this point of the book, I wanted to reassure you that it is not a disability and can have many benefits. Start this journey by becoming aware that you have different methods of learning and processing information. You may already know what they are.

You may be reading this book because:

You want to finally fit in and find your place in the world?

You are ready to find ways to move beyond the unique way your mind works and enjoy everything the rest of the world seems to take for granted?

You can be anyone and anything you want to be, provided you find a proven approach to managing your stress, anxiety, and anger that often feels like it's taking hold of you. The problem is that no one has taken the time to show you what to do until now…

DBT Skills for Mental Health is the book you need to read when you're ready to step off the sidelines and enjoy everything the big wide world offers. You will find advice, guidance, and motivation like never before, all in a neurodivergent-friendly way that allows you to take on board new ideas at your own pace. You may be super creative and visual, and there are exercises for you to help learn in your own unique way that you will find helpful.

You are going to learn about:

- Mental health and mental disorders
- Neurodivergence
- The benefits of DBT principles in preserving mental health
- Managing social anxiety in neurodivergent using DBT principles
- Managing stress using DBT and stress management skills
- Managing depression using DBT principles and positive psychology
- Managing anger using DBT principles and anger management techniques
- ADHD in neurodivergence
- Practicing emotional regulation
- Tips for a happier, mindful, and a more emotionally stable life

To get the benefits of this book, read through it carefully so that you understand the concepts described and complete as many of the exercises as you can. Take your time, there is no rush, and there is a lot of information to take on board. Some techniques and exercises have been repeated to help you learn more effectively. As I said before, everyone is unique, so do not try and compare yourself with anyone else. Whatever way you approach this book will be the right way for you.

Transformation

There are three important things to consider to change:

1. Awareness
2. Acceptance
3. Change

Before we can change, we need to become aware of our behaviors and emotions, that is the same for everyone, and this book will take you on a journey to help you to change and become more mindful. Awareness sometimes can be hard because you have to look more deeply into what is happening, but awareness is the key to change. Acceptance can also be difficult, but finally, when you learn new ways to accept who you are and your condition, this can be exciting. You will learn more about yourself, which is exciting but also can be challenging. Therefore, don't worry if you get stuck on awareness and acceptance; this is natural, but stick with it, follow the exercises, and when you have completed the book, you can reflect on what has worked and what hasn't.

From the moment you get started, you will find this book is accessible and designed to open your eyes to how your mind works. It's about celebrating what makes you different while equipping you with the skills and strategies needed to feel like you finally fit in with the rest of the world. Don't forget, your mental health condition is not a disability; you just need to understand how your brain works and find strategies that work for you.

WHAT YOU WILL LEARN

This book teaches you about emotional regulation and how to effectively manage your emotions to live a more emotionally stable life.

This is a roadmap for neurodivergence that includes DBT skills, stress management skills, anger management skills, and self-care practices that will help you flourish and truly be your own authentic self.

By following this guide, you will be able to:

- Unlock your highest potential
- Achieve your deepest desires
- Have a more emotionally stable mind
- Understand yourself better

HOW WILL YOU FEEL?

This book is designed for you to think more independently about what is happening in your life right now. It will help you move forward with confidence, no matter your challenges. You will feel in control that you have the right strategies in your toolbox to manage your feelings and emotions healthily.

This book will remind you that no matter what your challenges are at the moment, there is a way to manage them and live the life you want.

HOW TO USE THIS BOOK?

This book is divided into three parts. The first part focuses on mental health, mental illness, neurodivergence, and DBT principles for mental health. The second part discusses managing social anxiety, stress, and depression using tools like DBT principles, positive psychology, thoughts monitoring, and stress management skills. The third and final part of the book covers managing ADHD and anger using anger management skills and DBT principles and how to improve emotional regulation.

At the end of every chapter, there is a Roundup section to help you quickly identify the DBT steps and a quick overview of each chapter. We will go into more detail about the four DBT steps, but they are:

1. Mindfulness
2. Emotional Regulation
3. Interpersonal effectiveness
4. Distress Tolerance

Firstly, let's start by understanding what mental health and having a neurodivergent condition mean. Mental health conditions have been discussed extensively over the last few years, especially with COVID-19. Many people are struggling, but what does *mental health* actually mean? Let's break this down in the next chapter and dissolve any myths you may have heard.

PART I

MENTAL HEALTH ISSUES AND DBT

1

WHAT ABOUT MY MENTAL HEALTH?

ccording to the World Health Organization (WHO):

> *"Mental health is a state of well-being in which an individual realizes their own abilities, can cope with normal stresses of life, can work productively and is able to make contributions to their community."*
>
> — WORLD HEALTH ORGANIZATION (WHO)

This is an interesting statement because that means that we all suffer from mental health as we live our lives. Life can sometimes be difficult, but how each person navigates these challenges will be different. Whether you have been diagnosed with a neurodivergent condition or not, it doesn't matter because we all process information differently. What exercises or information may help your friend may not be the one that will change you.

MENTAL HEALTH; WHAT'S THE FUSS ALL ABOUT?

Mental health and mental illness are two different things but generally can be treated the same. The difference is that mental illness is a mental health condition diagnosis by a psychiatrist or other professional doctor. You may already have a diagnosis of ADHD, anxiety disorders, or depression. If so, these need to be professionally treated.

Whether you have mental health or a mental illness, the information and exercises in this book can help you, but obviously, it does not substitute for any professional help you are currently getting. If you are having suicidal thoughts, then please reach out to somebody. There are some great ways to get help at the end of this book.

Let me tell you that there is no shame in standing up and claiming that you have a mental illness. It is common. Let's look at the statistics.

The Stats

According to WHO:

- 1 in 7 10 to 19-year-olds experience mental disorders which are largely untreated. These include depression, anxiety, and behavioral disorders
- 3.6% of 10 to 14-year-olds experience emotional disorders
- ADHD affects 3.1% of 10 to 14-year-olds

1 in 7 experience untreated mental disorders! Wow, that is a pretty high statistic. Don't be the one that goes unnoticed and untreated; it can be treatable. As I said before, awareness is key to any kind of change, so telling someone that you might have a mental illness means that you are aware of what is happening to you. This will make you feel in control rather than feeling overwhelmed.

Signs that you are Suffering from a Mental Illness

There are many symptoms to look out for. This is not an exhaustive list, so please add anything you feel you are suffering from.

- Feeling anxious
- Excessive worrying
- Feeling depressed or unhappy
- Emotional outbursts
- Quiet and withdrawn

- Problems at school
- Problems sleeping
- Inability to cope with daily problems
- Unusual behavior
- Changes in behavior or feelings
- Lack of appetite
- Lack of motivation
- Feelings of unnecessary panic
- Withdrawal from friends and activities
- Tiredness and low energy

As you can see from the list, there are many ways in which you might be feeling. Your body, however, is your number one go-to for information; see your body as your own personal computer. Your body knows exactly how you are feeling and will give you the information you need if you just listen and be mindful. The exercise below will help you tune into your body to get information about how you are feeling.

Exercise

Find a quiet place to sit. Breathe in and out and ask your body: How am I feeling right now?

Are the feelings sitting in your stomach? Are your shoulders tight? Do you feel twitchy and unable to sit still?

Breathe in and out.

When you have the answers, get out a piece of paper and colored pens. Draw a mind map of how you are feeling or highlight the feelings you are feeling right now in the mind map below. Add more words to the empty strands below. This will give you a good starting point for where you are.

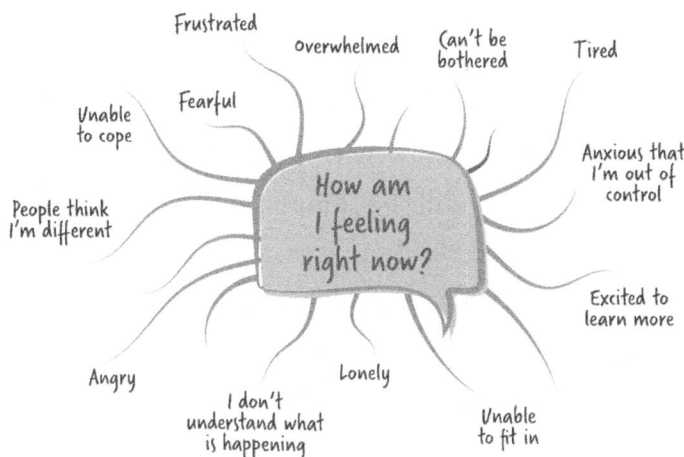

Your mind map might look like the above but don't worry or overthink this exercise. Just add words or draw pictures of how you are feeling. You are probably more creative than I am, so go wild with it. This is for your eyes only. You can share it with your parents if you want, but for now, this is simply for you to become aware of where you are right now. Do not judge how you are feeling; you are simply becoming aware and more mindful of transforming it.

Take time to do this exercise as you will be armed with useful information you can compare with after reading this book. It will be a great indication of how far you will have come, and this can be celebrated because sometimes we forget our journey when we feel better. For now, let's celebrate your honesty and courage in writing down where you are right now in your life.

ADOLESCENT YEARS

Becoming a teenager or living in this 21st century can be difficult for you, especially with the pressure that social media brings. There will be many changes at home, at school, and within your body that you might be feeling. You may be more aware of your feelings than you were before. Or, you may have suffered a trauma or been bullied at school, which will affect your mental state. Being a teenager isn't easy!

Consider that having a mental illness or condition now may just be a trigger of growing up, and you might need help to overcome the emotions you are feeling. Mental health doesn't normally fall out of the sky; there will have been a build-up of your feelings and emotions. When you feel stressed or overwhelmed, this is your body's way of telling you that it is worn out and can't take anymore. You have simply overloaded your computer, and it is screaming 'ALERT, ALERT!

If you imagine that each stressful event you have come across or emotion that is too difficult to process is a brick, and every single brick will then be used to build an imaginary wall, how tall do you think your wall is now?

When you feel overwhelmed and unable to cope, your wall is far too high. It wasn't just one event that caused you to go into overload; it would have been a build-up of many bricks over time.

How many bricks have you added over the years, months, and weeks? If you need to visualize what your wall looks like, then draw a picture of it now. Be proud that all your life experiences are now in every brick you have placed on that wall. Don't be frightened because if you knew how to build the wall, you could now unlearn those patterns. This book will help you live healthier so these bricks do not get built up again. You just need different information to break the wall down and keep it down. This is why change can be exciting. You just need new information for you to change and to live your best possible life.

RISK FACTORS FOR MENTAL ILLNESS CONDITIONS

Many factors will affect your mental health. For example:

- Trauma and abuse
- Loss of a loved one, such as a parent
- Neglect
- Changes at school

- Peer pressure
- Bullying
- Low self-esteem and confidence
- Moving home or school
- Not fitting in
- Diagnosis of a mental health condition; ADHD or Autism.

There are many more to consider. If you are struggling with your mental health, become aware of what things might have triggered your mental state. Do not dwell on them, just make a list, and you will be surprised at how many items you might be struggling with. I remind you that there would have been a build-up of stressors in your life; it didn't just fall out of the sky.

By being aware of the triggers, you can start asking for help in these areas. Also, finding a counselor or therapist will help you feel supported.

Most Common Mental Health Disorders

A wide range of disorders fall under the term 'mental health' and can be occasional or chronic. It is when your feelings, thoughts, and worries, and how you relate to other people, affect your daily life that you need help. More serious disorders will require professional guidance.

Here are four of them:

1. Anxiety Disorders

There are many anxiety disorders but simply explained, they are where the person has excessive thoughts about fear and worry that affects their behavior and life. These may include:

- **Generalized anxiety** – excessive worry.
- Panic disorder – excessive fear and feelings of panic.
- Social anxiety disorder – fear and worry about social settings (which we will cover in Chapter 3).
- Obsessive-compulsive disorder (OCD) – need everything in order, may have an excessive need to wash their hands, and have to perform rituals to be safe.
- Post-traumatic stress disorder (PTSD) – this is common following a trauma where they will relive that trauma and may have intrusive memories or flashbacks.

2. Depression - this is different from just feeling 'low'. The person will feel sad, irritable, and frustrated, and there is nothing positive for them in their lives for many weeks, months, or even years. They will have no motivation for anything and will feel sad and empty for nearly most of the day for many weeks.

3. Eating Disorders – this may involve not eating or eating and then making themselves sick. These people will be obsessive about the way they look physically.

4. Disruptive Behavior Disorders – these may be conditions known as ADHD and Autism. They are persistently disobedient and maybe violent. They do not abide by any rules.

DEBUNKING MENTAL HEALTH MYTHS

Here are 5 Myths to debunk:

1. Mental health is a sign of weakness

Fact: Mental health can affect anyone and has nothing to do with being weak. In fact, accepting you have a mental health issue requires courage and strength to ask for help and to change.

2. Mental health problems don't affect me

Fact: See the stats above. 1 in 7 10 to 19 years old experience mental health disorders that are largely untreated.

3. If a person has a mental health condition, they are considered stupid

Fact: No, mental health affects everyone. It is not a sign of high or low intelligence. It is more about emotional intelligence.

4. Poor mental health is not a big issue for teenagers. Their mood swings cause their behavior and they are seeking attention

Fact: It's true that adolescents have more mood swings because of their hormonal changes but may also struggle with mental health. It affects everyone at different stages of their lives. If mental health affects your life, it is time to get help.

5. There is no help for people with mental health issues. They are never going to get better

Fact: Many factors will help with mental health issues. DBT skills and also the suggested exercises will help you manage your mental health healthily. By learning new skills and managing your emotions and feelings, there is a lot you can do to get better.

MAINTAINING YOUR MENTAL HEALTH

There are ways in which you can maintain your mental health, and we will cover this in Part 2. Your diet, lifestyle, and how you express your feelings and thoughts all play a part. It isn't one thing that needs fixing or looking at; it will be a combination of factors you need to apply to your everyday life. Looking after your mental health is not a quick fix; it is a lifestyle change. You recharge your phone and look after that, but we forget to do the same thing about our bodies and minds. They also need to recharge to function how they should. If we feed our minds/brains with worry, anxiety, and unkind thoughts about ourselves, then no wonder that mental health is a problem in our society. If you look after yourself, exercise, eat healthily, have positive thoughts, and do not worry so much, then your mind and body will be at their optimum peak.

This book will teach you how.

In this chapter, you have learned more about what your mental health means to you; now, let's learn about what neurodivergence means.

> **Roundup**
>
> - Mindfulness — How is your mental health affecting your life right now? Tune into your body and ask: How am I feeling right now?
>
> - Emotional Regulation — Be aware of any emotional responses you might have at this time. Do not judge.
>
> - Interpersonal skills — Communicate your feelings and ask for help.
>
> - Distress Tolerance — Learn more about your condition and accept that this is where you are right now, and that is okay.

2

NEURODIVERGENCE EXPLAINED AND THE ROLE OF DBT IN MENTAL HEALTH

This chapter will give a deeper insight into neurodivergence; you will get familiar with the different neurodivergent conditions and what makes DBT a valuable tool when dealing with neurodivergence.

NEURODIVERSITY: WHAT IT IS AND WHAT IT ISN'T

Neurodivergence began with Judy Singer in 1998 when she discovered, from an autism perspective, that everyone's brain develops uniquely. It is a better way of saying 'normal' (neurotypical) or 'abnormal' (neurodivergent).

However, we must ask ourselves what is normal as there is no single definition of a 'normal' brain's function.

What it means is that neurodivergent people have different strengths and struggles from those people that are neurotypical.

Note that neurodiversity is not a medical term. It is a term used so that schools and work can understand that your brain works differently and how they can adapt to make things easier for you. Therefore, it is good to get a diagnosis because it will help you explain your condition which people will identify with in the long term.

COMMON NEURODIVERGENT MYTH BUSTERS

The neurodiversity movement is expanding, which is a good thing as people are beginning to recognize that this is a condition many suffer from. However, there is also bound to be negativity around this term, which may lead to some misconceptions. Those misconceptions have been borne by people not understanding the neurodiversity movement. Here are 5 Myth Busters that you may have heard.

1. The Neurodiversity movement is only about Autism

Judy Singer founded this movement, and the main focus was on Autism. However, this movement has expanded over time, and over the years has been realized that not just autistic people suffer from neurodivergence, but other mental health conditions also cover this. It is all about the inclusion of everyone, whether autistic or not.

2. Neurodivergent is a medical condition

Neurodivergent can cover many conditions and therefore are not recognized as medical conditions. The term helps others to understand the challenges of people with these conditions so they feel supported and understood. Neurodivergent can include anything from Autism, ADHD, Dyslexia, or anything classified as a mental health condition to brain injuries and trauma.

3. Neurodivergent people are not good at communication

Neurodivergent people struggle with normal social skills, but it doesn't mean they are not good at communicating. They just communicate differently. Understanding the way neurodivergent people communicate will help others to accept that no one form of communication is right or wrong.

4. The term 'neurodiverse' is just used to make people feel better

The term emphasizes the 'diversity' of the human mind and that these individuals need to be supported differently. The term helps schools and employers recognize that they need to adapt so people can thrive. It also advocates the strengths and weaknesses of neurodiverse people. Therefore, it is good to get a diagnosis and the help they may need.

5. High-functioning students are not technically neurodiverse

A common term neurodiverse people hear is 'high-functioning'. However, this label overlooks the struggles these neurodivergent people face.

The overall message of these five myths is that the term 'neurodivergence' allows others to understand the challenges these people face so school and work can adapt. Society can sometimes view this as a disability, but the message is that we should be an all-inclusive society, whether neurodivergent or neurotypical. By understanding this term, you will begin to embrace it to thrive in an inclusive world.

History of Neurodiversity

Neurodiversity was first mentioned in 1998 by Judy Singer, an Australian sociologist, when she wrote a sociology thesis. Neurodivergent became widely known when she later wrote a book called *Why Can't You Be Normal for Once in your Life?* Judy Singer wanted to dissolve the way people took for granted that all people functioned the same way. She wanted the term to represent a new addition to categories such as class, gender, and race. In her chapter, she said:

"Even our most taken-for-granted assumptions: that we all more or less see, feel, touch, hear, smell, and sort information, in more or less the same way (unless visibly disabled) – are being dissolved."

Judy Singer wanted the world to recognize the daily struggles of a person struggling with a neurodivergent condition. She also suffered from her own difficulties when growing up with obsessive behaviors; therefore, she understood what it was like to be different. She also suffered bullying and feelings of exclusion and faced challenges when building her career.

In 1998, when this thesis was published, Judy Singer was still ahead of her time. Harvey Blume first used the word 'neurodivergent' in the media, and then it appeared again in 2004 in the New York Times, and in 2005, there was a Neurodiversity/Autism Pride Day.

Since then, the phrase has been used to assist more people that have challenges with their brain being different rather than people suffering from Autism and ADHD.

NEURODIVERGENT CONDITIONS

Neurodivergence is often associated with the following conditions:

- Autism
- ADHD
- Dyspraxia
- Synesthesia
- OCD
- Sensory Processing Disorder

- Other learning disabilities
- Medical disorders

NEURODIVERGENTS, WHAT MAKES THEM TICK?

Here is an example of how neurodivergent people differ.

A neurodivergent person – Someone with Autism will struggle with socializing, but their strengths are their great attention to detail, a strong focus on skills, and creativity. They will learn better by having visual aids. They might have to have coping mechanisms when they socialize and maybe have a different strategy at school, i.e., more visual learning aids. They can draw or be very creative without attending lessons.

A neurotypical person – To build on their creativity, they may need drawing lessons, and working on attention to detail may have to be learned over several years. They will have a different focus on learning.

As you can see in the examples above, the two people are neither 'normal' nor 'abnormal', they just require different needs.

WHY IS A DIAGNOSIS OF NEURODIVERGENT IMPORTANT?

You might be worried that being diagnosed as a neurodivergent is negative. However, it can also be a positive thing.

Some people are struggling because it has not been recognized, and it will be harder for them at school. It is like having dyslexia; these people will need more help with reading and writing when diagnosed but will struggle if not. There is no shame; it just means you may learn or cope differently. Having a diagnosis will help teachers and parents to understand that your brain doesn't work the way it should, but your condition can be accommodated.

Once recognized, your school will begin to put things in place for you to have a more enjoyable time at school. These are some of the things they can help with:

- If you have difficulty with sensory overload, you may be able to work from home.
- Different ways of communicating that suit you.
- More time in exams.
- More support for managing time.
- You may be able to have a laptop or smartphone in the classroom to assist your learning.

Being aware of how you learn and how you are different will make life easier for you. A diagnosis is not shameful; it is there to help you and others understand your condition. Mostly other people don't understand why neurodivergent people are different; they just never considered it before, but the more information they have, the more help and assistance they can give you to support your learning. Others may be ignorant of your condition, but all they need is further information and understanding of how neurodivergent people tick.

If you become aware of your differences and have different coping mechanisms then later in life, i.e., when you start work or go to university, you will already be aware of how you work and learn better. This is seen as empowerment and not a weakness.

EMPOWERMENT VERSUS WEAKNESS

Consider this:

Do you want to feel empowered?

Knowledge is key. Be empowered now and have the coping strategies you need to live your best life. Don't let this diagnosis hold you back. Become aware of strategies that work, of how you like to learn, and how you can handle social situations that might be challenging for you. Whether you are neurodivergent or neurotypical, both can have challenges with your mental health. It is the way you deal with it that matters. Deal with it in a way that you feel empowered and not disempowered. Without knowledge, you are disempowered.

In this chapter, you have learned more about the term 'neurodivergence' and how it might affect your life. In the next chapter, we will look at what DBT is and how it can help you and your mental health condition.

Roundup

- Mindfulness – Be mindful of the different ways your brain works. What does neurodivergence mean to you?

- Emotional Regulation – How do you feel about having this condition? How does it affect your emotions?

- Interpersonal skills – Know about yourself more to communicate it to other people.

- Distress Tolerance – Sit with these feelings and don't try and change them. They may feel uncomfortable, but that is okay.

3

DBT (DIALECTICAL BEHAVIORAL THERAPY)

Dr. Marsha Linehan founded DBT. DBT is an evidence-based psychotherapy combining behavioral science with mindfulness and acceptance. It is useful to treat neurodivergent conditions.[1] DBT is a modified type of CBT (Cognitive Behavioral Therapy). The main basis of DBT is to teach people how to live in the moment, develop healthy ways to cope with stress, regulate their emotions, and improve their relationships with others.

The core function of DBT was to assist people with Autism, but it is now recognized to help with many other conditions that neurodivergent people are struggling with.

If you have been diagnosed with a neurodivergent condition, you might be struggling to understand and control your emotions, can't focus, and zone out. You may have challenges with social interaction and have inappropriate behaviors with strong emotions. The four major components of DBT tackle these challenges.

THE FOUR MAJOR COMPONENTS OF DBT

The four major components are:

1. Mindfulness
2. Emotional Regulation
3. Interpersonal Effectiveness
4. Distress Tolerance

We will delve more deeply into these four skills in the following chapters. You will also note that the Roundup at the end of every chapter focuses on these four major components to assist you in putting these four components into everyday situations that you might find challenging.

The benefits of DBT are:

- Identifying and labeling emotions
- Identifying obstacles to changing emotions
- Reducing vulnerability to the emotional mind
- Increase mindfulness of current emotions
- Strengthen emotional intelligence

Whether you are diagnosed with a neurodivergent condition or not, our mental health is something we all must learn to cope with. Sometimes life can be quite hard and navigating these difficult times will build your confidence in yourself. By using the DBT techniques, you will feel more in control rather than being controlled by your emotions.

If you sometimes feel that your behavior controls your emotions and how you think, these techniques will help you take yourself out of your emotions and see them for what they are.

There are also four stages of treatment with DBT:

Stage 1

Stage 1 is when you feel that your behavior is out of control. Your parents and teachers may struggle to help you; you may feel confused about your behavior being out of control. Your parents may take you to a professional person for therapy at this stage. You may be self-harming, using drugs/alcohol, and having feelings of suicide. This stage is to help you to achieve behavioral control.

Stage 2

In this stage, DBT will help you control your behavior, which is a great achievement. However, you will feel you are still struggling with life and suffering. At this stage, you may feel helpless and want to continue with DBT.

Stage 3

This is an important stage of DBT that will help you to live your life. It is all well and good to learn how to control your emotions and behavior, but this will give your life goals of self-esteem and confidence and how to define your goals in life. You will begin to learn how to improve your relationships with others. At this stage, you will feel at peace with yourself and your life. You will also feel happy, which is a good sign that DBT is working.

Stage 4

Some people will need this further stage, while others are already on the way to recovery and finding life easier and happier. At this stage, you may find that you have a sense of incompleteness and are not happy. You are looking to find joy and freedom, and at this stage, you delve deeper into the deeper meaning of what you want your life to look like and how you want it to feel. This stage will help you to experience joy and freedom.

As you can see from these stages, the more you learn about yourself using the four components of DBT; mindfulness, emotional regulation, interpersonal effectiveness, and distress tolerance, the more you experience joy and freedom. Stages 1 and 2 are all about learning more about your emotions and how to control them, and then Stages 3 and 4 will allow you to have a deeper meaning about yourself and what your life goals are.

The exercises in this book will take you through the whole four stages, but at first, you may find the exercises are only helping you to manage your symptoms. However, if you revisit the exercises, you may find that you might go deeper into who you are. By the end of this book, my hope is that you will have a deeper understanding of who you are and that you are ready to think more about your life goals than just managing your symptoms.

As you move through this book, look back at these stages to see where you might be on your journey.

THE ROLE OF DBT IN MENTAL HEALTH

The role of DBT in mental health will help you identify your distress, your emotions, and the kind of stressors, environment, or situations you might find challenging. DBT will give you the toolbox needed to navigate difficult times or everyday situations. You will feel more confident that you can control your mental health challenges and even teach your parents how to use DBT.

If you and your parents are all on the same page with guidelines and techniques to help you, then it will help you live your best life. You will find you can navigate life better if you have the right toolbox.

The Effectiveness of DBT

At this stage, you may be asking yourself why DBT works and whether it will help you. The reasons why DBT works are:

- It was created by someone with borderline personality disorder.
- DBT skills are easily taught.
- Emotional regulation skills are taught to help manage intense emotions without engaging in harmful or dangerous impulsive acts.
- Apply functional and applicable skills to various situations with ease and low cost.

In the following chapters, you will learn more about the four components and how these can be applied to manage your neurodiversity or mental health condition.

4

MINDFULNESS

Becoming mindful is one of the most valuable skills that will help you manage your mental health condition. Mindfulness is learning how to pay attention in the present moment without evaluation or judgment, to observe and *only* observe.

The word mindfulness has been branded over the years, but it is a simple technique that works well. Sometimes it is not easy to sit with your emotions because they can feel overwhelming, but by using mindfulness and focusing on your emotions, they can dissolve quite easily. It is when our emotions control us that life becomes difficult, and we feel out of control.

WHAT DOES BEING IN THE PRESENT MEAN?

You may have heard the term 'be present,' which means being in the moment, which is the basis of mindfulness. Being present every day may sound easy, but your brain is not programmed to just be fully present. We have been taught that multi-tasking is the way to go. Are you present now as you read this book, or is your mind wandering? Are you thinking about what happened an hour ago or worrying about what might happen in the future? Take a pause and see if you can be mindful of how you are showing up reading this book.

Mindfulness is being aware of what you are doing. For example, if you are washing a cup, stay in the present moment and wash the cup. Our minds tend to wander, and we begin to think about something other than washing up. Have you managed to walk to school without realizing what route you took? If you did, that means that you were not present; you were on autopilot.

Rather than being present, we worry about our day, what we say to people, and the past and future, and then our minds become very busy. It doesn't have a chance to slow down, to do nothing. Sometimes it can be quite scary when your mind is quiet because you are not used to it.

We need to begin to shut things out to stop the constant chatter in our minds. You might think you need to meditate or use any mindfulness techniques, and you don't have time or space to do that. Another effective way is by simply closing your eyes and shutting out all other sensory pressures; what you can see, what you can hear, and what you are sensing. By shutting out this information, you are simply focusing on nothing.

The beauty of mindfulness is that anyone can do it! It doesn't matter if you have a mental health illness or a neurodivergent condition; again, you just need to use the techniques that work for you. I will mention some helpful techniques, but please add anything to the list that you think would be useful.

Have you used mindfulness before? Has it been effective for you?

Mindfulness Techniques

These are some of the things that you can start to bring into your daily life:

- **Mindful breathing** – is where you focus on your breathing and nothing else. The exercises in this book will help you practice mindful breathing.
- **Guided meditations** – a teacher or another person guide you through a meditation. These are helpful if you find it difficult to sit quietly. These can be found online or on apps; Calm and Insight Timer are great apps to try.

- **Journaling** – is where you write down your thoughts and feelings. This will help you to process your feelings. You will learn more about journaling in the exercises throughout this book.
- **Gratitude journal** – is a specific journal where you write down what you are thankful for, allowing you to focus on what is good in your life. This will help you to take away the focus on being negative and make you feel more positive.
- **Body scan** – this is a mindful technique that allows you to tune into your body positively to see how you are feeling.
- **Mindfulness dancing** – dancing allows you to be free and express your feelings in a good way. Be mindful of how you are moving.
- **Mindful music** – music allows you to switch off and takes focus away from your negative thoughts and feelings. Be mindful and listen to the music and not as background music.
- **Walking** – is a good way to allow yourself to switch off and enjoy nature.
- **Jogging** – exercise is great for stress reduction and should be a part of your weekly routine.
- **Drawing** – this allows you to express yourself in pictures. Take time out to draw and be mindful. Focus only on what you are drawing and nothing else.

Some people perceive that you must sit down and meditate, but that is not true. If you find it hard to keep quiet for a period, try a walking meditation or dance. Being mindful doesn't mean you have to sit crossed-legged on a yoga mat; the key is:

To be aware of the present feeling and how you are feeling

Even dancing to music or walking can be a mindful technique. You might enjoy drawing or painting, and if you are in the present moment, engrossed in what you are doing, this is classed as mindfulness.

THE BENEFITS OF MINDFULNESS

As mentioned before, mindfulness is a great tool to become aware of how you feel and how your body reacts to your thoughts. These are some of the key benefits:

1. Reduces stress
2. Enhances performance
3. Increases awareness
4. Reduces anxiety and worry because you are accepting what is happening in the present moment.

Mindfulness is not a quick fix; it is a way of life, so it is important to use techniques you can use at home, school, or wherever you feel anxious or uncomfortable. Mindfulness is not just about picking one technique like meditation; you need to incorporate as many techniques as you can to fit every situation. I will talk about this later in this chapter.

Meditation

Meditation is a very good technique to help with being mindful as meditation begins and ends in the body. Meditation lets you drop from your head/mind into your body. Again, this is not as simple as it sounds because we are not used to listening to our bodies. We are used to being in our heads! Sometimes this can be frightening if you worry too much or have a lot of anxiety. However, the more you practice meditation, the more you will get used to the feeling of simply switching off your busy mind and relaxing.

Try this simple mindfulness meditation. It only takes 5 minutes.

Exercise: A Simple 5-Minute Mindfulness Meditation

1. Find a comfortable, quiet space to sit for 5 minutes with no distractions.
2. Sit up straight so that your breathing can flow more freely.
3. Focus on your breathing. Breathe in through your nose and breathe out through your mouth. Be mindful of how the breath feels as you breathe in and out. Is it cold? Is it warm? Notice how your body is feeling as you breathe in and out.

4. As you focus on your breathing, your mind may wander, and that is okay. Do not judge it or try to put any labels on your feelings. Just notice what is happening. Acknowledge that you may be feeling uncomfortable or you may want to move. Accept what you are feeling. It doesn't need to be perfect.
5. Keep breathing in and out and being aware until you are feeling calmer.

Try to practice this simple meditation for 5 minutes and then see if you can increase the time. Try 10 or 15 minutes and see how that feels. Is it any different from 5 minutes? This is a simple technique to help you with any situation that you might feel is challenging. This can be practiced anywhere to reduce anxiety and help you feel calmer. Practicing this technique will build your muscle strength by tuning into your breathing. Once your muscles are strong, it will be easier to do it when facing challenging times.

Knowing how and when you use mindfulness will help to retrain your brain. Our brains are pattern-matching all the time so if you have had a bad experience, let's say, at school, then your brain will use that as a template. Therefore, the next time you are in that same environment, the brain will say, "Ah, I was here before, and you felt panic." The body will respond to this pattern and turn on the panic/fear emotion. That is why avoiding a situation isn't a good thing. Learning how to cope with these situations is more helpful because it retrains the brain.

The good thing is that if you have trained your brain to do this, you are retraining your brain to do something else. How cool is that! Therefore, using the mindfulness technique will help you to cope with your challenging situations. If you are mindful and more relaxed, then it is less likely for your emotions to overrule your head.

In the next chapter, you will learn more about understanding and regulating your emotions and being more emotionally intelligent.

> **Roundup**
>
> - Mindfulness – Are you being mindful or not? Learn how to do an activity without thinking about anything else.
>
> - Emotional Regulation – Be mindful of your emotions in the present moment. Do not worry about the past or the future. What emotions are you feeling right now? Do you want to change them?
>
> - Interpersonal Skills – How can you use mindfulness techniques to help you understand yourself and others better?
>
> - Distress Tolerance – It is not always about changing your overwhelming emotions. Try sitting with an unsettling feeling, notice how it affects your body, and let it dissolve.

5

EMOTIONAL REGULATION

If you understand your emotions, it will help you to refocus on how you want to feel. Remember, awareness is key, so you must train regularly to keep control of emotions in any situation. Like your physical muscles, your need to build mental muscle strength to feel in control and stronger.

When you become a master at identifying your feelings and have strong emotional regulation skills, your mental health will improve significantly.

Emotions and feelings can be quite complex, and as you can see from the wheel below, there are many emotions and feelings. [1]

BAD AND GOOD EMOTIONS

In our society, we label emotions and feelings as bad and good.

What do you think bad emotions are?

What do you think good emotions are?

This is the wrong way of looking at emotions. Emotions are just emotions. They all need to be expressed, whether it is anger or happiness. Try not to label them as good or bad but look at all emotions that need to be expressed healthily. By not labeling them, you will not feel shameful or guilty when expressing anger or sadness. How you cope with them and express them is the important thing. If you don't express emotions, this can bring dis-ease into your body. There has been a lot of research to suggest that unresolved emotions can cause illness in the body. A lot of metaphysical practitioners work with emotions to try and resolve the dis-ease in the body.

A study conducted by Pennsylvania State University found that negative moods and emotions affect the immune system and cause inflammation in the body. By lowering the immune system, we are more susceptible to illness. That is why taking control of your emotions is important to your overall health and not only your mental health.

The Feeling Wheel can be very effective to try and identify what emotions you are experiencing. Sometimes it may be difficult to put the correct word to what you are feeling and experiencing. Therefore, this wheel will help you identify them quickly to find the right technique. The wheel will also help you identify a different emotion if you want to change the feeling you are experiencing. You can see that if you want to feel happy, then you can experience a range of other feelings.

Let's look at the yellow wheel 'happy' in the center. As you follow the yellow out into the outer circles, the emotions expand. Therefore, if you are feeling happy, you could feel 'playful,' and then if you look further into the wheel, it expands even more. It could be that you are feeling 'cheeky.' These will all fall under the 'happy' emotion. The wheel could help if you were unsure what emotion 'cheeky' is, then you can then relate it to the wheel and check that you are 'happy.' What a result!

If you are feeling 'withdrawn' or 'numb,' what would the emotion be?

Yes, that's right, 'anger,' but before you get to 'anger,' you could be feeling 'mad' or 'critical,' but it all relates to the emotion of 'anger.' Anger is just the breaking point at which you might become aware of it, but the more emotionally intelligent you are at identifying these emotions, perhaps you might be able to identify being frustrated before it gets to the point of anger, the breaking point.

REMINDER: Try not to label them as good or bad.

FEELINGS ARE JUST FEELINGS

Likewise, in depression, you may be feeling sad and irritable. If you then ignore these feelings, they escalate into a bigger emotion like depression.

What Are Emotions?

Many factors affect your emotional state. It could be your hormones, the weather, or whether it is hot or cold. Emotions are controlled by the limbic system that sits in the brain. It has three parts: the hypothalamus, hippocampus, and amygdala. A complex set of pathways goes to the limbic system for them to release the right hormones at the right time.

For example, if you were to see a tiger, the limbic system gets triggered, which will then flood your body with adrenaline to make you run. In this scenario, this emotion will save your life. Therefore, emotions and feelings can be useful and will trigger the right action.

Emotions are not useful when the limbic system fights the body's response to stress. It will keep going off like a doorbell. When your body is not in balance, these emotions will seem overwhelming, and you may act inappropriately.

When do you think an emotion might be useful in your life?

When do you think an emotion might affect how you live your life?

These are two good questions to take time to reflect on what the answers might be. Being more aware of when your emotions are useful and when they are not will help you to be emotionally intelligent. By being emotionally intelligent, it will help you come back into the present moment.

The feeling of love can be both useful and not. When you feel love positively, it is amazing, and you want more of it. But when that love disappears, then we are left feeling hurt. That is why it is not right to name emotions 'good' or 'bad' because all emotions can help you in your life. For example, if you are feeling happy at a funeral is it right to say that happiness is a 'bad' emotion?

It is all about regulating your emotions for the appropriate situations; that is it. So, if you are feeling angry, and it is hurting yourself and others, then this is not an appropriate action for that emotion to have. You need to be mindful of how you react so you can change the reactions to the emotions you might find challenging. Therefore, you can healthily express your emotions.

Emotions are a wise language, and when you learn how to identify your emotions and how they manifest in the body, then you will feel empowered that these can change. It is when we feel out of control that our feelings can be overwhelming.

How Can Emotions Affect You?

There are three ways in which emotions affect you:

1. How you experience an emotion
2. How your body reacts to the action
3. How you respond to an emotion

Emotions are sparked by sensations in the body and provide you with raw data, which is helpful if you listen to it. Emotions are sometimes not controllable because they can manifest either consciously (you are aware of them) or subconsciously (you are *not* aware, and the brain triggers these). Exploring how these emotions manifest in your body gives you great information on how to change.

If you think of overwhelming emotions as a warning sign and it brings a message, this will help you feel more in control if you understand why the emotion has been triggered.

An overwhelming emotion triggered in the body can be an unwanted feeling, but how you react to it is more important. You may act upon your emotions now unhealthily, and this is where you will feel overwhelmed and not in control. You cannot run away from your emotions; you will experience these feelings, whether they are wanted or unwanted. Running away from them will cause the body to respond with more unwanted emotions and panic.

These are some of the good ways in which emotions are helpful:

- Emotions help you to avoid danger
- Help others to understand your body through body language
- Help you to understand others if you are emotionally intelligent
- Emotions can prepare you to take action
- Emotions can motivate you to do things

How can you use your emotions so that they are helpful?

Showing your emotions and expressing them will help others understand you better. If you are closed to your emotions, people will find it hard to relate to you. Your mental health condition might affect how you show emotions, but you can still learn to be open. You can open up little by little and seeing your relationships with others improve will inspire you to share your feelings more with others.

Are Feelings and Emotions the Same?

You may have heard the words 'emotions' and 'feelings.' They are interchangeable words. However, emotions and feelings are not the same things. Feelings are experienced consciously, whereas emotions can come from the subconscious (you are *not* aware). This is great news because these feelings can be controlled. Feelings are generated by your thoughts and can increase by the stories we generate around these feelings, which are not necessarily the truth. Therefore, your feelings are not a truthful assessment of how you are feeling.

However, emotions are a more reliable source of information. Use this exercise to name the feeling.

Exercise

Sit quietly and place your hand on your body, either your heart or stomach. Tune into your body and name the feeling associated with your bodily emotion. Breathe in and out as this acknowledges that you are sitting with the emotion that will balance out the nervous system.

Ask what your emotions are trying to tell you. In what way could they be a useful signal to you?

Next, notice if you feel better by moving. Do you want to shake, stretch, or sigh? Moving your body or sighing releases the energy out of the emotion. Do not judge the emotion or feeling.

If you practice this regularly, then this will help you to regulate your emotions and feelings.

HOW DO YOU IDENTIFY YOUR FEELINGS?

Mindfulness techniques are a good idea to practice here so you can become aware of your feelings. Sit and be present with your feelings. If you are having trouble naming the feelings, use the Feelings Wheel or be present with how your body feels. If you are feeling anxious, you might have a tight chest, or, if you are feeling stressed, your heartbeat might be racing. Don't forget that you will have physical symptoms associated with these emotions, and if you begin to identify what emotions will trigger certain symptoms, then you have more information to begin to understand why these emotions are being triggered.

Try and fill out this chart:

Emotion	Physical Symptoms	My Thoughts	How can I feel better?
Frustrated and angry	Sweating, hot in the face, my legs shaky	I want to say something that will hurt someone I can't cope	Breathe deeply Sit with the feelings Smile and try and feel happy Move my body

Any kind of record is good whether you use the above or be creative with mind maps. You can then look back at it and see if you have coped better with the techniques shared in this book. You can then adjust your behavior to be more emotionally intelligent.

You can also share this record with your parents, teachers, or professional people trying to help you. When you are not experiencing these overwhelming emotions, it is hard to explain to others what you felt when the feeling has passed, and so you can show them this record, and it will help you communicate to them what help you need.

Learning more about yourself is a good thing because you can begin to change it if you want and have a deeper understanding of who you are.

Do Not Judge

By naming your feelings, you are just identifying the emotion, but **you are not** judging. If you are judging your feelings, then the emotion and feelings will get worse because you are installing a story behind the emotion. For example, if you felt anxious in a supermarket and then added a story behind that emotion, you will find going to the supermarket hard. Your brain would have recognized this is a pattern. The emotion of anxiety might not have been the supermarket but a symptom of you being stressed. Again, if you start judging emotions as bad, then the brain will remember the events and try to pattern-match the same feelings you had when you were in the same environment.

By accepting the emotion for what it is, just a feeling, then you are not falling into the story of the emotion. You are simply accepting happiness for happiness. Fear for Fear. There are no stories behind them to back those emotions up, which will make them worse.

Warning Signs of Emotions

Recognizing these emotions is critical to letting them go and changing them. When we ignore and repress these emotions, then they will grow stronger. It is healthy to express all your emotions. There is a saying that you get a slap in the face first as a warning, then if you don't listen, it will smack you around the head, and then if you are still not listening, you will walk into a brick wall.

It is this brick wall that we are trying to avoid. The brick wall is anxiety, panic attacks, and depression, so if we listen to the warning signs before we hit the brick wall, we are more likely to manage our emotions. The first sign might be that you are feeling frustrated or agitated, and the second sign might be overwhelming emotions of anger. If you accept your feelings at the first stage rather than ignoring them, you will not feel overwhelmed and out of control. The first sign is a slap in the face, asking you to listen. The second or later sign is your brick wall. The trick is to listen before you hit that brick wall.

Therefore, learn to be mindful and listen to the first warning signs. By practicing this, you will be less likely to hit that brick wall. You can manage the warning signs more effectively and quicker, but if you hit the brick wall, it takes a little longer.

Watch out for the warning signs; they may be subtle but practice listening to them. It will help you with your overall mental health, and you will feel more in control. Again, look at the Feelings Wheel to help you quickly to identify your emotions.

There are a couple of strategies that will help you remain in control.

Create a Safe Space

When you are expressing your emotions, it can make you feel vulnerable and unsafe, and therefore it is a good idea when you first start practicing expressing your emotions to create a 'safe space.' Firstly, start by expressing your emotions to yourself. Practice the technique above where you write down how you feel and want to feel. Even by writing down your emotions, they are technically out of your system so you are expressing them. Expressing your emotions is unique to you. The number one thing to remember is that for you to express your emotions freely, you will need a safe space to be in so that you feel supported and safe.

Physical Space

That safe space can be in your environment, so pick somewhere where you are comfortable. Find a quiet space to sit and write down your feelings and pick that space every time you want to express your emotions. This allows you to establish a routine, and your brain will begin to realize that this space is for expressing emotions like it knows when you want to sleep. As we have already established, the brain likes habit and pattern matching.

It takes 28 days to create a habit, so stick with it. At first, it can be challenging, and many distractions will take you

AWAY from your feelings. Be aware of this but also be determined that this is a useful exercise and you are doing it. If you want some motivation, take your favorite drink or food into that area with you and get comfy. Make it your space.

How do you want to feel in your 'physical safe' space?

Mind Space

Sometimes it is not possible to go into your physical safe space as you might be away on holiday or you might want to sit quietly when you are away from home. It is still possible to create a safe space in your mind. Where do you feel safe? Is it your space at home, or would you like to be on the beach with the sun beating down on you? It could also be in nature, sitting underneath a tree, so you feel supported by the tree's trunk.

Close your eyes now and create this safe space. See the colors of your space; is it hot or cold. Are there any noises, or is anyone else there with you? Be creative with this vision and make it bigger. It doesn't have to be based on reality.

Then when you want to express your emotions, you can close your eyes and conjure up the image of your beautiful, safe space.

How does your 'mind safe' space feel like?

SELF-TALK

Sometimes we create stories around who we are that are not true, and this negative self-talk will trigger unwanted emotions. If you feel bad about yourself, then you may experience negative feelings. Don't forget negative feelings are generated by negative thoughts.

Do you have a lot of negative self-talk going on in your head? This negative self-talk is sometimes known as the 'ego mind' or the 'monkey mind.' Have you heard either of these expressions?

When we are mindful and live in the present, this negative self-talk is not noticeable. Similarly, when we listen to music, we cannot hear this voice. However, when we are quiet, we can hear this monkey mind, which is mischievous and wants us to think that we are not good enough and can be very negative.

It is important not to listen to this self-talk as it is a part of your mind and not a part of you. They will mostly be negative thoughts about yourself and will be negatively forecasting. You will have 60,000 thoughts per day and listening and acting on these thoughts can be exhausting. A thought is just a thought until you put a story behind it and believe it is true. These thoughts are not true; they are just your monkey mind trying to be annoying. We have learned over the years how to talk negatively to ourselves, so we need to be mindful. Being negative about yourself every day, every hour, and every minute will increase your stress levels, and that is why it is important to either turn down the volume or not listen to it. You can try to be mindful of your thoughts, write them down and let them pass like a train through your mind. Try it and see how you feel.

Here is the most popular negative self-talk that you might experience:

- I am not good enough
- I am weird
- I am not normal
- I am rubbish at school
- I am ugly
- I am fat

Can you see how these statements begin with 'I am'? By telling yourself, 'I am ugly' all day, your mind will begin to believe this statement, and your body will react accordingly. Your mind is plastic, so you can mold it. Therefore, if you feed your mind and body with positive thoughts, you are retraining your mind to be more positive.

Positive Self-Talk

The more positive you are about yourself, the more likely you are to feel happy and at peace with who you are. We are all different, and we all are unique. Everyone has problems, and your problems might be bigger than some, but that is okay. That is who you are and needs to be celebrated.

What positive things can you say about yourself:

- I am positive
- I am doing my best
- I am a caring person
- I am loving

Can you feel the difference when you say the negative and then the positive words?

Exercise

Go back and read the negative self-talk statements and be mindful of how your body feels. What emotions are you experiencing right now?

Now read the positive self-talk statements. How do they make you feel?

Even if you don't believe the positive self-talk statements, it is good to practice saying them out loud. Again, trick your mind into believing these things. It is a good way to feel confident in being you, which will help you raise your self-esteem (how you feel about yourself).

Now that you know more about your emotions and how to regulate them, why not teach your family some techniques so that they know how to help you when you are having an outburst of emotions. Families want to help but sometimes don't know what to do, so communicating this to them will help you and them live happier lives.

In the next chapter, we talk about how you effectively communicate with yourself and others.

Roundup

- Mindfulness – Use the Feelings Wheel to identify your emotions. Do not judge. Keep a record.

- Emotional Regulation – Accept your feelings; they are neither good nor bad. Decide how you would like to change them.

- Interpersonal Effectiveness – Keep a record so you can effectively communicate how you were feeling in the moment to others.

- Distress Tolerance – sit and record these feelings. Do not put a story behind the emotion, as it will make it stronger. Anger is just anger; there is no story behind it.

6

INTERPERSONAL EFFECTIVENESS

In simple terms, this means how you communicate with others and how you interact well with other people. However, firstly you must be aware of the relationship you have with yourself; how you feel about yourself, and how confident you feel so that you can communicate better.

In this chapter, we will look at how you can improve your interpersonal skills and be mindful of how you communicate.

WHAT ARE YOUR CHALLENGES WITH YOUR COMMUNICATION NOW?

Be mindful of how you communicate with:

- Your parents
- Your teachers
- Your friends
- Strangers
- People in authority

We communicate differently with all kinds of people depending upon what level of respect we have for them. For instance, you will communicate differently with your parents because there is an emotional attachment of love than your friends or teachers.

Exercise: Over the next few weeks, keep a record of how you communicate with different kinds of people. It could look something like this.

	Who was I talking to, and where?	How did I feel before the conversation?	Did I listen?	What feelings did I have for that person?	After the conversation, how did I feel?
Monday	My teacher	Frustrated	No. I was thinking too much	Felt annoyed at my teacher	I was confused at how the conversation went
Tuesday					
Wednesday					
Thursday					
Friday					
Saturday					
Sunday					

Don't try and change anything yet; just be aware of the situation, who the person was, and how it made you feel. Even if you felt angry or frustrated, that is good. If you need to identify your feelings, then make use of the Feelings Wheel. Keep the wheel where you can see it so you can become more intelligent in identifying your feelings.

Listening versus Speaking

When we communicate with people, we think we need to speak all the time, but sometimes people just want you to listen to them. You may find this difficult.

When we communicate with people, our minds are actively pattern matching, so if your friend triggers off one of your internal buttons, then communication can be very difficult. Simply, your emotions get in the way, and you are coming from a place of hurt and anger. This is how aggressive communication can be triggered. However, listening and being mindful of how you are feeling and what they are triggering can be immensely helpful to you so that you can change how you react.

You may be finding it hard to socialize now, so by being mindful of how you communicate and your reactions, you will begin to enjoy socializing and feel at peace when you have difficult conversations with people.

Don't expect that all conversations are easy. Manage your expectations in that you are *going* to have difficult conversations and you are going to have *enjoyable* conversations. How you act is more important than the circumstances of the conversation.

Don't forget we communicate in different ways:

- Face-to-face communication
- Emails

- Telephone
- Texting
- Presentations
- Written communication

Let's make it more simple:

HOW YOU EXPRESS YOURSELF IS A FORM OF COMMUNICATION

Therefore, in whatever way you express yourself, these tips and techniques will help you.

Having a Relationship with Yourself

Although how you express yourself is a form of communication, it is also important to be aware of how you relate to yourself. If you have low self-esteem (how you feel about yourself is negative) then it will be more difficult to socialize and listen to other people because you will feel that you are being attacked or put down. That may not be the person's intention, but because you feel low about yourself, this will affect any communication.

Self-Esteem

This is how you 'feel' about yourself. Do you have negative thoughts about yourself? Here are some signs of low self-esteem:

1. You don't like yourself.
2. You feel you are not good enough.
3. Comparing your abilities with others.
4. Having negative thoughts about your abilities.
5. Criticizing the things you do.
6. Don't like the way you look.
7. Can't seem to fit in.
8. Can't bear to look at yourself in the mirror.

You can always change these thoughts about yourself. You can decide whether you want to put yourself down or not. It is up to you, no one else. What decision do you want to make? Do you want to change?

These are some signs that you have high self-esteem:

1. You like yourself.
2. You feel you are good enough for whatever life brings you.
3. You are okay with the way you look.
4. You are mindful of what you say to yourself.
5. You are willing to change the things you don't like.

Decide now how you would like to feel about yourself. Be in total acceptance that this is who you are, even your flaws and that you feel confident in being you.

Confidence

Most people think that self-esteem and confidence are the same things. They are not.

Self-esteem is an inside job.

Confidence is an outside job.

What does that mean? It means that confidence is built with the things that we do externally. If you are not a confident flyer, flying around the world will help you build your confidence.

It is a doing thing and not a feeling thing.

You might think you were born lacking confidence and, therefore, you can't change. You may also think that your best friend has more confidence than you, which is how they are. It is not. Confidence is learned and must be practiced.

Exercise

Write a list of the things that you are confident about. It may be drawing, playing games, walking to the shop, or speaking to your friends.

Then write another list of what you are not confident about. Do not judge, this list will vary from person to person.

Maybe you are not confident about speaking to strangers or not confident about cycling to school.

Just be mindful of these things, and don't try to change them just yet. This will also help you know your strengths and weaknesses, which we will discuss later.

HOW TO IMPROVE YOUR INTERPERSONAL SKILLS

There are three ways to improve your communication:

1. Active Listening
2. Empathy
3. Emotional Intelligence

Let's look at these more closely.

1. Active Listening

When was the last time that you listened properly to your friends, teachers, or parents? Were you mindful of what was being said, or were you busy being angry and frustrated that you had to communicate?

Active listening is the most important tool for improving your interpersonal skills. Sometimes it is not all about talking and expressing your own feelings; it is about actively listening and not being attached to the conversation.

Here are some ways in which you can actively listen:

- Don't interrupt
- Don't judge
- Focus on what the person is saying
- Don't plan on what to say next
- Don't impose your opinions
- Don't try and create a solution

2. Empathy

If you go back to the awareness list you did earlier, look at who you were talking to. Consider that the person you were talking to had their own issues they were dealing with on the day you spoke to them. Perhaps they were feeling vulnerable and angry or having a bad day. By understanding how the other person is feeling, you will be able to empathize with that person more effectively. You may find it difficult to pick up on the feelings of others, but there is no harm in asking. You could say: "Are you angry because of what is going on with your other friend?" Or, "Why are you feeling sad today?"

The number one issue of breakdown in communication with others is that you take on board that they must be angry because of YOU. You take what they are saying to you personally. We all do this to some extent because of our lack of self-esteem or how we are feeling on that day. When we are lacking in self-esteem, we do feel that it is our fault! That is why we become angry, defensive, and frustrated because we feel we are being attacked.

Think about the other person. It is not all about you. Your friend or teacher may be having a difficult time that day or feeling unsure, and you can help them by understanding and being aware of their feelings. Empathizing with other people will help you maintain distance from your feelings.

Remember: it is not all about you!

3. Emotional Intelligence

Emotional intelligence is a fancy word for being self-aware. We spoke before about managing your emotions; it is the same thing. Below is a list of someone with emotional intelligence:

- Self-awareness – knows themselves on a deeper level, including their strengths and weaknesses.
- Empathy
- Social Skills
- Well placed boundaries
- Getting along with others
- Recognizing how others feel
- Being confident about who they are

We have already talked about most of these, and by reading this book and becoming more aware of yourself, your emotional intelligence will increase.

This quote by Socrates sums it up:

> *"To know thyself is the beginning of wisdom."*
>
> — SOCRATES

As I said before, you can only change one thing, and that is yourself, but to do that, you need to know yourself.

Exercise

Be mindful of how you can increase your emotional intelligence. Pick one thing from the list above and commit to being mindful and how it affects you and the other person.

For example, if you picked 'getting along with others,' spend an hour in your day being mindful of that. Go to school and see if you can get along with the most annoying person or if you can get along with your teachers. Be mindful, and then make a list of how you were feeling.

Give yourself a pat on the back in whatever way it goes. Smile and remember that you can always practice being emotionally intelligent another day.

Here are some tips to help you communicate effectively.

Introducing Yourself

If you know you get nervous when meeting new people, a good tool would be to practice how you would introduce yourself. You can practice this with your parents and good friends and see how you feel about introducing yourself. Being armed with this script will give you confidence when you normally feel nervous in social settings. Nerves and fear can override your thinking process, so we likely forget what we need to say. Have you been in a nervous situation where you can't remember your name? Then you know how it feels when you are nervous, but practicing this script will be easier to remember, and you can reel it off.

Here is an example:

Morning! I don't think we've met before, I'm … How are you?

I like to swim after school. What do you like?

I don't like English. How about you?

Exercise

Try it for yourself.

- Draw a mind map or write a short paragraph to introduce yourself.
- Sit in front of a mirror and be mindful of how you feel when introducing yourself. Don't forget the first time you will feel uncomfortable, but the more you do it, the more confident you will feel.
- Keep repeating number 2 above until you feel more confident and good about introducing yourself.
- When ready, try it out on your parents and close friends. Don't ask for feedback; just simply be mindful of how you are feeling.

As you can see in the example above, asking questions will take the pressure off you, and you can then actively listen to their responses. This can also give you a bit of breathing space, so you don't have to keep talking.

It's Not All About What you are Saying

Body language is also important when you introduce yourself. People notice not only the words you speak but also your body language.

Top tips for body language:

- Smile
- Stand up straight
- Look at the other person. If eye contact is uncomfortable, then just smile but look at the other person's face.

Here are some simple tips to keep you confident even when you don't feel like it.

Responding to Praise or Compliments

This sounds simple but receiving praise or compliments can leave you feeling vulnerable. Have your friends told you how good you are at sports? How did you respond? I can guarantee that you probably batted it away and said something like, "No, I'm not. Ross is much better than me." This is a sign of deflection because accepting praise or compliments shows you are vulnerable and open.

Also, if you have low self-esteem, this will affect your response. A compliment might boost how you are feeling, so accept these compliments. It will help you when you are feeling low about yourself. Don't forget if you feel that your friends are feeling low, you can give them a compliment to make them feel happier.

How do you respond to a compliment?

All you need to do is say, 'Thank you,' and smile.

Responding to Negative Feedback

It is not what people say to you; it is how you respond to the situation that you can change. I keep saying it, you can only change one thing, and that is you. If you try and change other people, it just doesn't work because it is not in your control.

If you look at the Control Wheel below, you will see what is in your control and what is not.

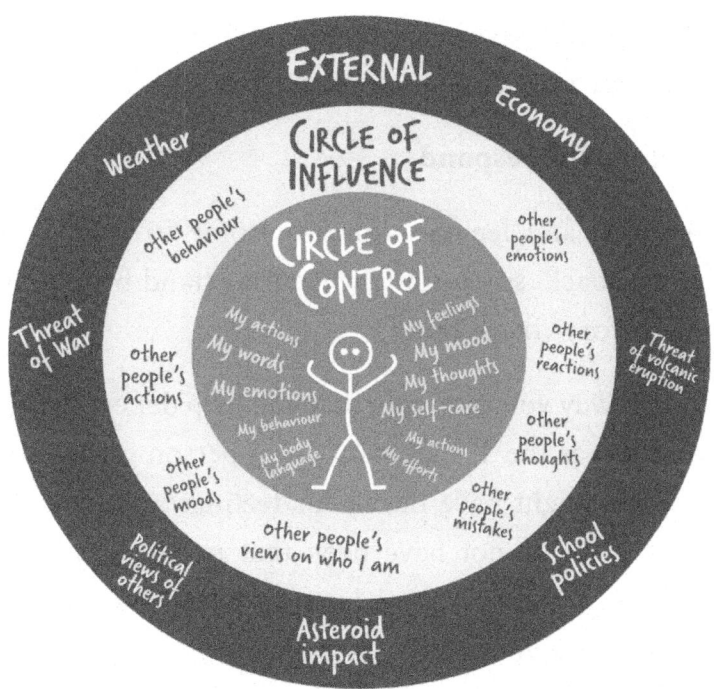

We cannot control anything outside of ourselves, so any change that needs to be done will have to come from inside us. As you can see from the diagram above, you can change:

- Your words
- Your tone
- Your thoughts
- Your kindness

Therefore, when responding to negative feedback, you can control your words and thoughts. Normally when people or friends give negative feedback, it comes from their own opinions and life experiences. Sometimes it is never about us, but they are projecting their negative stuff onto us.

Think before you respond

Our emotions and feelings can also come to play in this negative feedback, so you might need to stand back a little and think before you respond.

There is one way you can reply that will help deflect the situation, and that is the 'I' statement. That person giving negative feedback might have hurt your feelings and made you angry, but it might not have been that person's intention. Therefore, responding: "I feel hurt by what you said," will help you to take ownership of your feelings.

This also deflects the situation because you are not accusing that person of anything. It only gets into an argument when you say: "You *made* me feel sad." This is a different statement to use, and the other person will probably become defensive and say, "That's not what I meant at all. You always take a negative approach."

Can you see the difference?

Using the 'I' statement, you can control your feelings and emotions over the situation and help you feel in control.

Being vulnerable

Being yourself is not easy because it means you need to be vulnerable, that you are open and honest about who you are and your feelings. Vulnerability is not a sign of weakness; it is a strength. Below is a list of how you can practice being vulnerable.

- Voice your feelings. Don't be afraid to say when you are happy, sad, or angry.
- Do not take on board other's opinions of you. They are their opinions and have nothing to do with you.
- Try and avoid being perfect. Life is messy and doesn't go to plan, so plan for the unexpected.
- Be open to new experiences.
- Be willing to forgive.
- Be willing to admit when you are wrong.

Most importantly:

- Be in the moment – be mindful and do not judge yourself or others.

That is why recognizing your feelings is important so that you can tell the other person exactly how you are feeling if you feel upset and hurt by what they are saying.

Exercise

Make a game out of being vulnerable. Firstly, learn how to be vulnerable with your family or close friends. Tell them you are trying to change your responses and play roles in certain situations with them. Make a game out of it, and you will begin to learn to have fun and laugh at situations.

For example:

Mum – I am really angry at you because you haven't done your homework.

You – I am sorry you feel like that, but I have done as much as I can. I need some help in completing it.

Mum – Okay, what help do you need?

This is a sign of being open and honest. You are communicating effectively and being honest that maybe you haven't done your homework, but you have tried and are willing to accept help. This is a good example. Rather than getting angry with your mum and telling lies, it is okay to be open and honest. Practice this with your close family and see what responses you get. Have fun.

To sum up, interpersonal skills are how you ask for what you want in a positive way that will help you with your self-esteem and confidence. It will help you build positive relationships with others. Be mindful of how you interact with yourself and others.

In the next chapter, we will talk about how to endure pain in difficult situations and not change it but be mindful of it.

Roundup

- Mindfulness – Be aware of how you communicate with different people and yourself. Only say positive things to yourself.

- Emotional Regulation – Be aware of how compliments and praise make you feel and take the appropriate action.

- Interpersonal Skills – Commit to changing your response and rehearse 'no' responses. Use the 'I' Statement to help you with negative situations. Build your self-esteem.

- Distress Tolerance – Can you sit with unwanted feelings when people upset you? How can you manage your overwhelming emotions?

7

DISTRESS TOLERANCE

There might be times when you become overwhelmed with emotions and feelings, and your body will go into a state of panic. This is where distress tolerance plays a part because you are not trying to change your feelings. When overwhelming feelings appear, your first instinct is to run away from them. You may become agitated, unable to sit down, and feel unsettled because you feel overwhelmed by your feelings and how your body responds. Your system becomes overloaded, and you are unable to cope. Your body is flooded with adrenaline, and that is why it is difficult to try and change your feelings. You are on high alert, and your body is reacting to this. You may have physical feelings in your body. You may feel unable to breathe, you may feel tightness in your chest or you have a headache. All these feelings are normal when you are on high alert.

Don't forget: ***Feelings are just feelings***

Sometimes these feelings give us a message, which is a good thing because we can begin to change how we respond to them in the future. It might be because your brain is pattern-matching to certain situations, and you haven't done anything at all. It might be that you have lots of negative thoughts, and your body has responded to feeling overwhelmed.

Distress tolerance is how you manage any intense emotions without feeling overwhelmed. Again, be mindful of why you have these intense feelings rather than letting your mind spiral into further emotional outbursts. Being aware of your distress tolerance will also help you to manage your stress healthily. An unhealthy way could be that you run away from these intense feelings or distract yourself by self-harming or taking alcohol and drugs. By ignoring these feelings, they will keep coming back until you identify with them.

SURVIVAL

When you have intense feelings that make you panic and want to run away, it is about surviving these feelings without making them worse. Acceptance is a good tool because you are just thinking:

I'm just feeling panic, and that is okay.

Rather than thinking:

OMG, I'm feeling panic! I need to get out of here; what if I can't cope?

Can you hear the tone in each of them? The first one feels calm. The second one takes you into more panic, which will then bring on more intense unwanted feelings. In this instance, when you are feeling overwhelmed, it is about the survival of the fittest. You will get into trouble when you try and avoid these feelings.

If you are feeling overwhelmed and can't cope, here are some things you can do at the time.

Improving the Moment

Do not forget that we are not trying to change anything, so these tips will help improve the moment you feel these intense feelings. Try and practice them when you are calm because then you will remember what to do when these feelings appear. You will then feel confident that you can cope in the moment and will not fear them. These intense feelings can appear through fear; we fear they might appear the next moment. Be confident that you can cope and that these feelings will indeed pass. They might only last for one or two minutes, but it will feel longer, but they will pass. It is how you cope in the moment that will bring you relief and will build your confidence for the future.

Acceptance

One technique that will help you survive these overwhelming feelings is just by sitting down, feeling them, and accepting them for what they are. Do not judge the feelings; they are neither good nor bad. They are just feelings. Remember that nothing will happen; you will not die or be ill by having these overwhelming feelings. You can ask for help from someone that might understand your fears. By accepting these feelings, you will not make your feelings worse and will reject any fear you may have.

FEAR is just False Evidence Appearing Real

Fear is not real. You may have these intense feelings of fear that something might happen and feel uncomfortable in your body. You feel like running away, but nothing will happen if you just sit down and be with them. Let me tell you that it is not as easy as it sounds because you will have a flood of adrenaline that sometimes prevents you from being still, but if you repeat the saying – False Evidence Appearing Real, this will calm you down. It is when you buy into your fear that it will spiral out of control.

ACCEPTS

One of the DBT techniques is ACCEPTS:

Activities – Engage in an activity that distracts you from your feelings.

Contributing – Focus on other people, not yourself. Volunteer and do a good deed for someone else.

Comparisons – Compare the situation you are in with a worse one. Remember a time when you were in more pain.

Emotions – Do something that will create the opposite feeling. If you are feeling anxious, listen to calming music.

Pushing Away – Push your negative thoughts away. Write them down on a piece of paper and then throw the piece of paper away. This will help you to release all of your negative thoughts.

Thoughts – Try and focus on your thoughts.

Sensations – Wear a rubber band and snap it on your wrist to distract you away from your intense negative feelings.

Another DBT tool is Urge Surfing which you will find at https://www.therapistaid.com/worksheets/urge-surfing-handout with other great exercises.

Do Not Beat Yourself Up

This is one thing that you need to be mindful of because you will make those unwanted feelings worse. Beating yourself up is when we have negative internal thoughts about ourselves. We continually make our feelings worse by saying negative things when we should be kind to ourselves. Therefore, when you are feeling overwhelmed, you may say to yourself:

OMG, I'm not normal.

Why is this happening to me? It must be me making it worse.

It is all my fault.

I must have done something wrong.

There is something wrong with me.

This is just negative self-talk and is not helpful at all. Accepting your feelings means you are not judging them or putting yourself down. Think about this for a moment; even when you say something negative to yourself, you are metaphorically beating yourself with sticks. Put the sticks down. Rather than beating yourself up, be kind and gentle with yourself.

SELF-SOOTHING

Be kind and caring to yourself. As before, don't think negative thoughts about why you are having these feelings. Be gentle with yourself and love yourself even more.

A mindful technique is to meditate using all five senses; see, hear, touch, taste, and smell.

Mindful Meditation

Sit quietly and focus outside of yourself rather than inside.

1. Use your eyes to see what you can see; look at the textures and colors of your environment.
2. If you are sitting, feel what the seat feels under your legs or think about how the clothes feel on your skin. Touch something in your environment, like a windowpane or the sofa. Be mindful and sense how those feel.
3. Focus on your mouth to see if you can taste anything. Or eat a small amount of food and be mindful of how that feels in your mouth. Does the taste remind you of anything?
4. Breathe in through your nose and see what smells you can pick up. Do they remind you of a particular time or event? Are they pleasant smells?

Focusing outside of yourself will be helpful to distract yourself from overwhelming feelings. Remember that feelings are just feelings, and they can't harm you unless you allow them to.

Below is another form of distraction that will take your focus away from your unwanted pain and feelings. Practice this when you are not feeling overwhelmed to see how it feels both when you are in a panic and when you are calm.

Distraction

How do you distract yourself from these feelings now? Here are some suggestions:

- **Music** – playing soothing music will help your mind to focus on the music and distract your mind from focusing on your feelings. It will also quieten down the negative internal chatter in your mind.
- **Talking** – find a good friend and chat about anything other than your feelings. This is good when you are feeling anxious when traveling. Before you finish your conversation, you will be at your destination.
- **Exercise or walking** – this is good because if you are feeling overwhelmed and have lots of adrenalin in your system. When this happens, you may find sitting down, being quiet, and meditating hard, but that is okay. If so, walking or exercising would distract you from the feelings. Exercise will also manage adrenalin as exercise will flood your system with the good feeling hormone, dopamine.

WHAT ARE YOUR EMOTIONS TELLING YOU?

As previously mentioned, your emotions are feeding you good data on how you are and what your body needs. If you identify with what the messages are, you will be able to find the right action for the appropriate message, and this will stop you from feeling overwhelmed.

Ask yourself the following questions:

1. Are these emotions giving me a message?
2. What are the positives to feeling these feelings?
3. What appropriate action can I take?

Remember, we are not trying to change these feelings; we are being mindful of why they occur and what messages they are telling us.

Perhaps the message is that your body is tired and needs to exercise. Or that your body goes into a panic when you are in certain situations. This is a positive message because you know that this is an area you need to work on.

Keep a Record

When you are outside of these intense feelings and feeling calm, it is sometimes difficult to remember what happened. You may feel that you were being silly for not coping or that you cannot now think of why you reacted in the way you did. You are not being silly, and you did cope, but keeping a record will help you keep track of these feelings at the time. They will also help you be more mindful of these certain feelings' messages.

Here is an example:

Date	What were the feelings?	How did I cope?	What were the positives of these feelings?	What did I learn from them?	How can I react differently to them in the future?
1/12/22	Sad	I shouted at my friends	I noticed that I needed some quiet time alone	It is okay to be sad	Next time I will just tell my friends that I need some quiet time

Remember that the brain pattern matches so this is a good exercise to try and retrain your brain not to react in these situations. Thereby you are changing these reactions for the future as you learn more about them but are not changing them now.

Don't forget:

You've got this. You are strong enough to cope

In this chapter, you have learned what distress tolerance is and how to manage stress healthily. Sometimes intense feelings will appear whether you are doing something stressful or not, but it is more important to manage these feelings and try not to change them. The techniques I have shared with you will help you cope with these intense situations, and maybe the next time you have the same feelings, they will not be so intense.

Now that we have learned about the four DBT techniques, in Part 2, we will look at how to apply these techniques to help you to manage social anxiety, stress, and depression.

Roundup

- Mindfulness – Use some techniques to help you survive; accept, distract, or make a list of the positives of that emotion and how you coped. Be aware of any messages your feelings are trying to tell you.

- Emotional Regulation – Accept your feelings at the moment. They are not good or bad; it is just as it is. Are they acceptable emotions for the moment, or do you want to change them?

- Interpersonal Skills – Learn more about yourself to communicate effectively with others. Raise your self-esteem and learn to use your body language to communicate.

- Distress Tolerance – Do not try and change your feelings. Just sit with them and survive. Remember, survival of the fittest.

PART II

COMPREHENSIVE DBT APPROACH: SOCIAL ANXIETY, STRESS MANAGEMENT, AND DEPRESSION

8

MANAGING SOCIAL ANXIETY IN NEURODIVERGENTS

In this chapter, you will learn all about social anxiety and how to manage it using DBT principles.

Do you worry a lot about going into social settings? Is it disrupting your life?

We all have some levels of anxiety when we are experiencing new things or challenges, but when it disrupts or causes us problems in our lives, we need to look at what is causing our stress and how to manage it.

SYMPTOMS OF SOCIAL ANXIETY

You may have or have experienced the following symptoms:

- Sweaty palms
- Blushing – going red in the face
- Nausea
- Constantly worrying about going into a social setting

When you are trying to avoid any social setting because of fear, it is time for you to do something about it.

What is Social Anxiety?

Social anxiety is when you struggle with social situations. If you have been diagnosed with ADHA or Autism, then this is a common problem. However, social anxiety can be an issue for most people. Being mindful of how you interact in social settings will help you manage your expectations and the expectations of others.

Social anxiety is a form of anxiety disorder. According to Mental Health America, an estimated 31.9% of adolescents between the ages of 13 to 18 had a form of anxiety disorder. 38% were females, and 26% were males. As you can see, you are not alone in having an anxiety disorder.

Is it More than Shyness?

You may be thinking that you don't like social settings because you are shy or an introvert (someone who likes their own company). You keep telling yourself that you like your own space and don't get on well with people. To live your best life, socializing and interacting with other people is an important aspect of your life. From school to making friends and when you go out into the wider world of work, the expectation is that you will have some form of social interaction. It is time to look at it now rather than leaving it because in time, if you are not aware of it, the fear will grow bigger.

Being an adolescent is difficult as there are many changes to your body and social settings. It is time to become more independent from your parents and family and to do it alone. This can be a scary time for most adolescents, especially if you are neurodivergent and have a condition like ADHD or Autism. Social anxiety is common in adolescents because you may become more socially aware, and your peer groups at school and home may have different expectations from you.

Therefore, it is not a question of whether you are shy or an introvert; it is about dealing with your fear and being mindful of how you react to these fears.

Fear

Fear is what drives all anxiety conditions, but if you remember the acronym:

False **E**vidence **A**ppearing **R**eal

This puts fear into perspective. Fear kicks in when there is a threat to harm, whether imagined or real. This tells us that the brain doesn't know whether it is reality, and this is the key. If the brain doesn't know reality from fiction, then we can trick it into managing fear. Social anxiety is when fear kicks in while you are in social situations. By managing this fear, you can look at social anxiety differently.

You might have had an awkward or embarrassing moment in a previous social setting, which may have increased your fear about going into that situation again. Next time, before you go into any social situation, you can imagine a different scenario to help reduce your anxiety.

Exercise – Imagine a Positive Scenario

Try this exercise and see if it makes a difference.

Imagine yourself going into a room full of strangers, you take a moment to look around and find yourself smiling. You stand up straight and may feel a little nervous, but that is okay. The room is bright and noisy, but you can turn the noise down like a radio. You feel confident. Strangers approach you, and you shake their hands. You introduce yourself and smile. They are friendly people, and you enjoy meeting new people.

When doing this exercise, see what difference it makes to your feelings and body language. Don't forget it is not all about verbal communication; body language matters, which is why standing up tall helps you break free from fear. Beating fear is just building up muscles as you would in the gym by using weights. Re-programming your mind and having some tools in your toolbox before, during, and after the fearful situation you are approaching will help you feel more confident.

It is not about avoiding fear because this will worsen as it grows and grows until it is disproportionate to the actual situation. Have you ever told your friends a story that has gotten bigger and bigger than the actual event? This is how our minds perceive the situation. It will keep growing and growing until you face your fear.

Therefore, it is time to become mindful of why these situations are challenging and stressful and learn some techniques to trick your mind.

Why Do I have Social Anxiety?

It is relatively unknown why people have social anxiety, as many factors exist. However, these are a few that might help you identify:

- Fear of talking to strangers
- Fear that you look anxious
- People will stare at you if you feel you are different
- Fear of people's expectations of you in social situations
- Your own expectations
- Childhood trauma

Can you identify with anything on that list?

Overall, fear is the last message that kicks in when your stress levels are high. We tend to think that if we have had a bad situation in a social setting, we begin to feel that situation is what triggered our fear and stress. However, if you consider that maybe you had a bad day at school, argued with your teachers, and then had to meet new people, your stress levels are already high, and meeting new people will have tipped it over the edge into anxiety and fear. Fear and anxiety are the last messages, the brick wall, but you would have received messages before that. That is why it is important to listen to the messages.

How Do You Feel about Yourself?

Self-esteem again plays a part in this level of anxiety because if we feel rubbish about ourselves, we perceive that others will think rubbish thoughts about us. Do you admire anyone, a TV personality or movie star? If you do, try, and see how they act on screen. See their body language and how you think they might feel about themselves. If you do the exercise above about positively imagining the next social setting, you can imagine being in their shoes. How does that feel?

Being self-assured will help you in any social setting, and you won't worry about what others think. When you are unsure of yourself, you then worry about what others think.

If you can't remember anything else when the overwhelming feeling of fear kicks in, then do two simple things:

- Stand up straight, and
- Smile

Try them now. Put the book down, stand up tall, and smile. How do you feel?

Fear of People's Expectations

There is a saying to remember:

> *"What other people think about you is their business and not yours."*

If you take a look at the Control Wheel in Chapter 6, it will remind you that you cannot control what others think about you, and therefore it is a waste of your energy worrying about it. As I said above, we worry about what others think because we feel inadequate in ourselves, which we are projecting onto others. This is something you are in control of, and you can change. You can change:

- Your thoughts
- Your emotions
- Your way of handling situations

You cannot control anything else; you cannot control other people, and you cannot control situations. The only control you have is yourself! This is really good news because you know that you can be mindful of yourself, be more self-assured and learn techniques to help you in certain situations.

Are You a Perfectionist?

Worrying about meeting people's expectations is normally a sign that you are setting too high standards for yourself. Perfectionism is when you want to appear perfect to everyone.

These are some of the signs to look out for:

- High personal standards
- Criticism of self and others
- Highly critical of yourself
- Focusing only on results
- Setting unrealistic goals
- Feeling depressed that you haven't met your goals

This is all driven by negative self-talk and low self-esteem, which we have already discussed. It is important to be mindful of this because it will raise your stress levels even more. It is about trying to minimize your life's stress so you can live your best life. That is why self-esteem and being mindful of what we say to ourselves are *very* important to master.

Perfectionism might become a problem in social settings because there is a fear of judgment attached to perfection. You will become driven by appearing to be perfect, there is nothing wrong with you, and you are trying to fit in. That is the wrong way of going about it because it is simply not you.

Raising your self-esteem so that you feel great about yourself will help immensely with social anxiety.

MANAGING SOCIAL ANXIETY USING DBT PRINCIPLES

There are a few DBT skills that you can try. Remember, it is not a quick fix. Practice the techniques to see which one works well for you.

The DBT skills ask you to take the opposite action to your feelings. If you do the same thing, you will get the same results, which is why you need to be mindful of not doing the same thing repeatedly. You might want to run away or avoid the situation, but this will not help.

Below are the top tips on how to manage your social anxiety healthily.

Self-Soothe

When you are in social settings, be kind to yourself. You may feel anxious, and that is okay. You may feel unsure of yourself, and that is okay. Be gentle with yourself and know your limits. If the social setting becomes too much, ask for help or leave and take a breath. By being kind to yourself, you can be mindful of your needs rather than letting fear take over.

Mindfulness

Use this exercise to prompt you to write down how you felt in certain situations and what you learned from it.

Date	What social setting was challenging for me?	How was I feeling before the event?	How was I feeling during the event?	How was I feeling after the event?	What did I learn from that situation?
30.11.22	Going to the shops	Feeling tired	Challenging, too many people	Irritated and frustrated	To go shopping when I am not feeling tired

Writing down things also helps you get them out of your head and is a form of expressing your emotions. As I said before, your mind will keep replaying the event repeatedly until it is really bad when in reality, it might not have been that bad at all. You might have felt a little anxious, but you coped. It will help you to put your feelings into proportion. Remember to do this exercise before and after the event to capture the real essence of your feelings.

Remember also to remain in the present moment. Don't worry about the past or the future; just be there in the moment. It will be enjoyable and a further step for you to change. Try not to think about past social situations where you didn't feel like you were coping. You have more strategies in your toolbox now; you understand yourself better and react to emotions more healthily. Therefore, you are not the same person as before, which is good news because how you would have reacted in the past is not how you will react now or in the future.

Emotional Regulation

In Chapter 5, we discussed your emotions and how to use the Feelings Wheel to understand your feelings. When you first think about social settings and even going to school, what is the first feeling that you experience? Fear might be the first feeling, but as we know, fear is not real, so look beyond fear and see exactly what the feeling is.

DBT RAIN TECHNIQUE

The acronym RAIN is an easy-to-remember tool for practicing mindfulness and compassion using the following four steps:

R = Recognize what is happening.
A = Allow the experience to be there, just as it is.
I = Investigate with interest and care.
N = Nurture with self-compassion.

We have used exercises in this chapter to help recognize what is happening, allow the experience to be, investigate it, self-soothe yourself, and give your compassion. By remembering the acronym RAIN, you can remember to put all these things into action.

The above exercise is some of the DBT skills that you can apply but remember that every small step you take to overcome your social anxiety will break the cycle in the future. It may be difficult at first but look at your long-term goal of feeling confident in these situations. Don't forget you are retraining your brain.

Social anxiety is another thing that will raise your stress levels; therefore, managing your overall stress levels will help you in your long-term health goals. In the next chapter, we will look at how you recognize and manage your stress.

Roundup

- Mindfulness – Mindfulness is the go-to technique. Be mindful when you are in difficult situations and record your emotions.

- Emotional Regulation – Accept that you might get anxious in social settings. Be mindful of your emotions when you are in those situations and look to see what strategies you can use to change them in the future.

- Interpersonal Effectiveness – Think about what techniques you can use before, during, and after a challenging situation and also how you can have a better relationship with yourself.

- Distress Tolerance – Learn techniques on how to survive difficult social settings without making the situation worse. Don't change the situation but learn from them.

9

MANAGING STRESS IN NEURODIVERGENTS

Stress occurs in everyone's bodies or thoughts in different ways. What stresses one person will not necessarily stress another. You might like to fly, but your friend may find it very difficult to sit on a plane and, therefore will get stressed out.

Your body, mind, and hormones do a great job of regulating your body. Your body knows what to do when you are out of balance because it will secrete more hormones to regulate your body. That is their job. However, sometimes there is too much interference in this process from you, your environment, other people, and your thoughts.

For example, imagine a bucket by your side and all your stresses as water. Think of everything that is challenging and maybe stressing you out. You might be stressing about a test at school, a meeting with a friend, or having to do something difficult that you might not be happy about. Add to that bucket your condition, like being neurodivergent, having ADHD, or Autism. These conditions will also add stress to your body and mind. Add any other trauma that you might have had. Now imagine your bucket getting full up. Add everything that you can think of. I bet that your bucket is now overflowing!

Your body will cope with a certain amount of stress without you even realizing it, but when the bucket is overflowing, your body will go into 'overload,' and that is why you might experience overwhelming emotions and have unwanted feelings in your body.

Normally your bucket is emptied when you sleep, and that is why sleep is so important. However, some days your bucket does not get emptied, and then on the next day, you are adding more and more stressors. Can you now see how stress does not just come out of the sky; there will always be a build-up? There might be one thing that will tip you over the edge, but it is not **that** thing. That is why it is important not to judge the situation where you might feel extra stressed or emotional because it might not be that situation; it might just be that your bucket is too full.

Stress is a warning sign that your body is on 'overload'; it can't simply deal with any more stress. However, if you need to learn to catch these warning signs before they get out of control, they are more unmanageable. Look for the little signs that your body and mind need attention before you get overloaded.

STRESS IN NEURODIVERGENTS

If you have a condition like ADHD or Autism or are diagnosed with a neurodivergent condition, unfortunately you have much more cortisol (the primary stress hormone that regulates your body's response to stress). That is why you must learn to manage your stress.

- The more neurodiverse you are = the more stress
- More stress = more relaxation and managed techniques needed

As I said before, do not try and compare yourself with your friends or other neurodiverse people because we all manage stress in different ways. Now that you know that people like you tend to have more cortisol, you are armed with the information to change. Building stress management techniques into your life will make life easier for you to manage your stress.

Stress is Not Always Negative

Stress can also be positive because:

- It helps you stay motivated
- It can inspire you

- If you fail a test, you will be more motivated to do better

Therefore, it is not all bad news. However, you need to learn to manage stress healthily.

What Are the Signs?

Everybody experiences stress in different ways, but here are some to be mindful of:

- Significant emotional changes

- Changes to academic performance

- Unexplained physical issues like:

  - Aches and pains
  - Headaches and migraines
  - Stomach problems

- Sleeping problems

- Anxiety or panic attacks

- Social problems

- Changes in general behavior

Mindfulness is a great tool to help you tune into your body to identify how stress affects you. You can use the Body Scan Meditation below, which will allow you to scan your body, identify your feelings, and see what is going on in your body.

These symptoms are similar to those experienced by people suffering from ADHD and Autism.

GUIDED MINDFULNESS TECHNIQUES FOR RELAXATION

Meditation

Mindfulness meditations are a great way to calm down your nervous system and for the hormone dopamine to be released. Do you remember that dopamine is the 'good feeling' hormone we discussed earlier? This is the hormone that makes you feel happy. Also, by closing your eyes, you are shutting out all the stimuli, and this is particularly useful if you have sensory problems. Just close your eyes and shut the world out for a minute or two.

Here is a mindfulness meditation to help you pause and be mindful of your body.

1. Body Scan Meditation

- Find a quiet place where you will not be disturbed. Close your eyes if you feel comfortable doing so.
- Take a deep breath in.
- Breathe out and feel your body relaxing.
- Focus on your breathing. Is it shallow? Is it quiet? What is the texture of your breathing?
- Next focus on your chest. How is your chest feeling?

- Focus on your shoulders. Are they tight? How do they feel?
- Tune into your arms. Move them around and see how they are feeling.
- Move down and focus on your stomach. How is that feeling? Tune in and see if you can see any colors. Are there any feelings stuck in your stomach?
- Move down and focus on the tops of your legs. How are they feeling today?
- Move down and focus on your legs. Are they heavy?
- Ask your body: what do I need?
- Take a deep breath in.
- Breathe out and journal any answers that you may have received.
- Open your eyes if they are closed.

If you find it difficult to keep focused throughout the entire body scan, start focusing on a few parts of the body. You can then build up to a whole-body scan when you are ready. Every time you do this exercise, it will become a little easier. It doesn't have to take long, and when practiced, you will be able to scan your body in a few minutes. Just do as much as you can. This technique allows you to take a moment to tune into your body and to be mindful of how you are feeling.

Using this technique will make you more aware of how stress is appearing in your body. At this stage, we are not trying to change anything. We are just noticing. We often do not notice that we are stressed because when we feel excited and busy we have a lot of adrenaline which makes our body move more. It might be difficult to calm down, so you will have to choose the right technique for you. That is why it is important in this meditation to ask your body what it needs.

Your body is super intelligent and knows what it needs to regulate to keep you healthy. Your interference in this process will make it harder for your body to regulate. Also, we do not listen or haven't been taught how to listen to our body's messages, and we overload it with more stressors. Be kind to your body; it is an intelligent computer and will let you know when things are wrong if you listen and treat it well.

2. Take Deep, Mindful Breaths

Our breath is our powerful tool, but we forget this as it is a natural occurrence, and we do not have to think about it. Concentrating on your breath helps calm the nervous system and relaxes your whole body. Be mindful of how your breath feels as it leaves your lungs and fills your nostrils. Breathe out through your nostrils. Place a hand on your belly and see if that goes in and out with each breath. If not, then you are shallow breathing through your chest. Practice and see if you get the belly to go outward when you breathe in and inwards when you breathe out. Try and see what your belly does.

Or you can try this 7:11 breathing technique:

Sit somewhere quietly and close your eyes.

Breathe in for seven counts

Hold

Breathe out for eleven counts

Simple. It is effective; you just need to breathe in less than you breathe out. Try it out and see how it feels. Do you feel calmer? Can you manage to hold your breath? Is it difficult to breathe out for eleven?

3. Practice Mindful Journaling

You have been doing a version of journaling already in the previous exercises when you have written the results of being mindful in situations and how you are feeling. Why not practice journaling every day? You can write about your feelings or whether things went well or didn't go well. You can draw pictures or mind maps or simply write down a few words that are meaningful to you. By getting your emotions out onto paper, you are expressing your emotions and will feel less stressed. Try journaling for a week to see if you are feeling any better.

4. Listening to Soothing Music

Keeping a quiet calm mind can be difficult when your head is racing with worrying thoughts, so listening to soothing music will help you tune out those thoughts. Get some noise-inducing headphones and when you are feeling frustrated or overloaded, put them on and listen to some soothing music. Sometimes listening to the waves of the sea or nature sounds are good to soothe your nervous system.

5. Guided Visualizations/Meditations

If you find it difficult to meditate on your own, guided visualizations or meditations are great. There are many free guided meditations that you can access. Insight Timer is a great tool and one you can have on your phone to listen in any situation in which you may need help to calm down.

TIME MANAGEMENT TIPS FOR A STRESS-FREE DAY

Prioritize

Managing stress is not all about being calm and breathing; it sometimes involves more logical thinking and taking appropriate actions. You may feel overwhelmed by the number of things you need to do or think about, and when it is all in your head, the tasks seem bigger than when you write them down. Writing them down or making a checklist will help you with this process. Try this exercise if you feel overwhelmed with what you need to do.

Exercise

Use this table as a guideline to help you to prioritize. You might want to draw the table and use different colored pens and be more creative, but the principles still apply. Below is an example for you to see how it works.

Task	Do now	Schedule and do it asap	Ask someone else or delete	Delete / Not important at all
English homework		It is due on Monday – leave it until then		
Making my bed	Do it now. Easier than worrying about it.			
Tidy my room			I can ask my mum to help as I am feeling overwhelmed	
Being mindful	It is important as I am feeling a little stressed. Do it now!			
Play my game				Not important, I can do this another day when I'm feeling better

Switch Off Your Mobile Phone

, this adds to our overall stress levels. We simply don't have time to be quiet. Our brains are taking on information all the time. Thereby sometimes we have to stop this information overload and stop checking our messages on our phones for a time. Switch them off!

This will help you to focus and be present. You can simply be and take some time out. Read a book or go outside in nature.

Stay off Social Media

For young people, social media plays a part in adolescent life, and sometimes not in a good way. Our culture is based on FOMO – fear of missing out, and one where you think everyone is having a good time and feeling happy. This can leave you feeling inadequate and could lower your self-esteem. Having a set time off social media can help you manage your stress levels, so try to have an hour or two off social media regularly throughout the day or week. Set the time in your diary when you can be reminded. Be mindful of how social media makes you feel when watching things and when you have time out. Tune out all the information that might be your triggers.

Don't Multi-task

As a society, we are often told that multi-tasking is a great quality to have, but this is not being mindful. We are trying to do too much at any one time, which can cause your brain to go into overload. Focus and be mindful on one task at a time, get that one finished, and then start another one. Use the chart above to prioritize your tasks so you do not have to worry about forgetting to do any.

Self-Care Practices

Don't forget that you are an important part of your stress levels and having a few self-care practices under your belt will help you to feel more positive about yourself. Low self-esteem (how you feel about yourself) is not a healthy way to manage your stress so do things that raise your self-esteem. Below are a few suggestions.

Positive Self-Talk

We have mentioned this before, but positive self-talk is important to remember. Be kind and considerate to yourself. Saying bad things about yourself is like eating sugary snacks all day and is bad for your health. Saying positive things helps you to stay motivated, and you will feel happier. Don't forget that your mind can be tricked even if you are not happy as it cannot distinguish between what is real and what is not. You can do this by saying positive things to yourself.

These can be:

I am doing my best

I am learning new things, and I am proud of myself

I love myself even when I make mistakes

These are all positive self-talk messages that your brain will love. Negative self-talk will add more stress to your system, which isn't good for your overall stress levels.

Sleep

Sleep is very important because this is where your bucket is emptied and dealt with in a deep sleep. If you do not have enough or intermittent sleep, then your bucket is never emptied; therefore, the next day, your bucket will be over-filled before you even get up. Be mindful of how much sleep you need because, as a teenager, you might need more sleep than your parents. There is a lot of change in your teenage years, both physically and mentally, and therefore you need extra sleep so that your body can cope with it.

A good technique is to have a bedtime routine. No, this isn't just for babies and toddlers; it is good practice for everyone. It is no good playing on your computer, speaking to your friends, and then getting into bed thinking that you will sleep. Your mind will still be very active, so it is not as simple as that; you need to calm your body down first and tell your brain that it is time to sleep. Below is a good bed routine to follow. Everyone goes to bed at different times, so first, be mindful of what time suits you.

A Good Bedtime Routine

At least an hour before your optimum time for bed, switch off all your electrical screens. The light on any screen will keep your mind active, and the hormone that switches on for sleep will think it is daytime and not time for sleep. The hormone melatonin is released with darkness and tells our body it's time to sleep. This is why being around too much bright light before bed can affect our sleep, as it can stop the release of melatonin.

Turn your mobile phone off, so you are not distracted by it.

If you need to be active, read a book or something that doesn't involve a screen and light.

A bedtime drink is a good way of telling your body that you intend to sleep soon. You might find an herbal tea will help your body relax. Try not to drink or eat any sugary things that will keep you feeling awake.

Have a hot shower or bath and put on your favorite pj's.

Snuggle down in your bed. Not too hot but comfortable for you.

Try and play some soothing music or listen to a sleep meditation.

Close your eyes and relax.

Doesn't that sound good? It may take a bit of practice to calm your mind down but stick with this routine. Be kind to yourself and self-praise yourself for trying. Every little behavioral change will help you in the long term. It is not a quick fix. You must learn and practice the techniques that work well for you.

Exercise

Exercise is a great way of releasing the adrenaline in your body. If you are stressed and find it difficult to calm down, then any type of exercise will help you. When you exercise, dopamine and serotonin (the good feeling hormones) are released into the body, which will help lower your cortisol levels (stress hormone). This will help you calm down and make you feel happier.

What exercise do you like to do? Do something that you like because it is easier to stick to. There is no wrong or right answer, so take a pause here and consider what you like to do. It can be walking, running, playing football, going to the gym, or anything that will keep you active. Sometimes when you exercise, your mind will quieten down, and you will be able to forget your worries and enjoy the exercise.

If you are not used to exercising, find something you like. Don't be disheartened if you try running and don't like it. That's okay. It is good because you are mindful of what works for you and what doesn't. As I said, there are no wrong or right answers to this; it is all about being self-aware, in control of what you want, and being confident with your decisions.

What Do I Like to Do?

Another mindful technique is to be engrossed in an activity you like. This will help you to feel motivated and inspired.

The exercise below will help you to discover what you enjoy doing.

Exercise

Try and list as many activities that you enjoy doing. For example, listening to music, running, painting, walking, or being in nature. Write words or draw pictures that will help to remind yourself of what you enjoy doing.

This mind map will help get you started. Insert more activities that you like doing in the empty threads.

Challenge

I challenge you to commit to doing one of the tasks you enjoy weekly. Be mindful and journal how you felt, how easy or hard it was, and did you enjoy it.

Doing activities that you love to do will make you feel happier and therefore reduce your stress levels. You can do things with others or by yourself, which is fine. If dancing in your bedroom makes you feel happy, then do it. You might enjoy painting, writing, or solving problems. If that is what you love to do, then do it. Don't question whether this is helping your stress levels; it is because when you are feeling happy, the 'good feeling' hormones are released. Even the simple fact of smiling will help you to release these hormones.

If you are struggling to find something you like to do, be mindful and present when undertaking these tasks and see how you feel. Make a list of things that made you smile and laugh and things that didn't. Experiment and ask your parents or teachers to help you suggest things if you are struggling. Try new activities and see if they make you smile and make a note of whether you liked them or not. Make it a fun game and get everyone involved.

Any of the above techniques can be challenging for neurodivergent people, so again, pick the ones you feel comfortable with. Practice them when you are calm and stressed, and be mindful of how you feel.

If you have a short attention span, do the above techniques in short bursts. Don't be worried that you are not doing them right and they are not working. They will be working for your overall long-term mental health, and sometimes you do not notice any immediate change. Stick with them because you have the courage to try new things to change.

10

MANAGING DEPRESSION IN NEURODIVERGENTS

Think about anxiety and depression as being on one line, anxiety is on one side of the line (worrying about the past), and depression is on the other side (worrying about the future); you are either worrying about the past or the future. That is why most exercises you have already completed for anxiety will also help with depression.

If you are feeling sad, you will be unable to see what your future will look like, and this can feel overwhelming, and therefore you will retreat into yourself. This can also be part of your mental health condition, so be careful, as it can be misdiagnosed.

WHAT IS DEPRESSION?

Depression is a long-term feeling of sadness, so if you are just feeling sad for a few days, that is not depression. It is when these feelings affect your life that you need to seek help. This feeling can be very difficult to manage as you will lack the motivation to do anything. Even getting out of bed will be difficult.

Depression is a mood disorder that can affect how you think, feel, and act. If you are depressed, you will have a strong feeling that life isn't worth living. Have you ever felt like that before? Are you feeling like that now?

People have this misconception that if you are feeling low, you can simply 'snap out of it,' but this isn't the case. This is a mental health condition and not just simply feelings of being low. You may need to seek professional help. Talking to others will also help you to feel that you are not alone. Depression is a common mental health condition and is becoming more common, particularly during COVID-19.

Signs that you are depressed:

- Lack of motivation
- Feeling sad
- Outbursts of crying
- Lacking in energy
- Unable to focus
- Withdrawn from people

- Unable to perform simple tasks without feeling sad
- Seeing the negatives in everything
- Feeling worthless
- Poor performance at school
- Not sleeping
- Self-harming
- Feelings of anger

COMMON CAUSES OF DEPRESSION

The number one cause of depression is loneliness. If you have been diagnosed with a mental health condition, this might leave you feeling isolated and lonely, and you may feel like no one understands you. You are trying to deal with a lot, and the common reaction is to retreat and isolate yourself from others. At this stage of your life, you have a lot to take on board but isolating yourself is not a healthy way to cope. Yes, you need time alone to know who you are, but you also need support. If depression is a problem for you, it is time to communicate how you feel with others and get the help you deserve. There is no shame and guilt about how you feel because it is treatable, and you can get help. Using the techniques in this book will help you too.

You may feel 'why me' and 'why is this happening to me,' but communicating your feelings to others will allow them to understand your condition and how they can help. They cannot help if they don't understand how depression affects you. You are not alone in your condition, as many people are struggling with depression. However, you are the strong one because you have been brave enough to learn how to manage it.

If you think you may be depressed, you might need specific therapy to deal with this. If you have thoughts about self-harming, then you must seek medical advice. Do not suffer in silence; it is always better to deal with these things when you first notice them, as it will be easier to deal with. Speak to someone and get the right help.

If you think about depression in that you feel overwhelmed with sad emotions and have simply unplugged from life, this chapter will help you to plug back in. That is why you feel you can't be bothered with simple tasks, can't be bothered to communicate, and can't see any positives in anything. You may also feel like you are in a dark tunnel and can't see a way out. These emotions can be scary but don't worry, as there are things you can do. You can manage depression if you are aware that this is what you are suffering from. Be confident that you will be able to feel happier about your future when you learn more about how to manage depression.

Depression in Neurodivergent People

In neurodivergent people, depression may feel different. As you are already mostly experiencing unusual sleep and eating patterns, you may have low moods, which can be mistaken as part of your condition and not depression. Therefore, it is very important to be mindful of seeing if those patterns change. The patterns of feeling depressed may increase in intensity, so you must be aware of any changes you are experiencing. That is why keeping a diary or journal of your feelings is very helpful to identify if anything changes or increases. Also, if you struggle to communicate how you feel, you can show your journal to the people you trust to help them understand.

TIPS FOR MANAGING AND PREVENTING DEPRESSION

If you feel you can manage your depression on your own, here are some techniques to handle these emotions healthily.

Mindfulness

Let's revisit the 'How am I feeling' map mind.

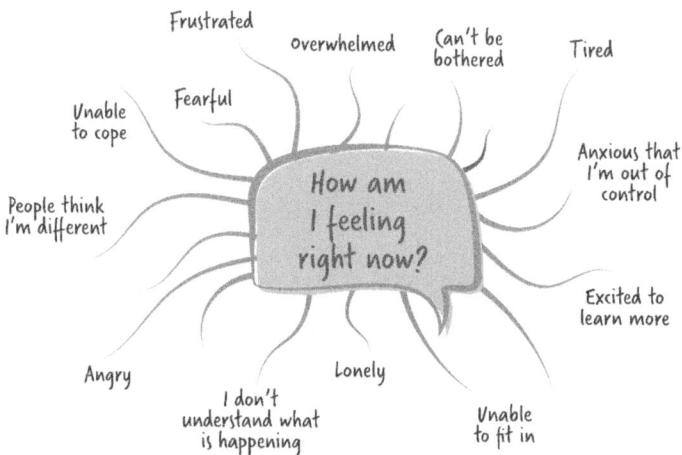

Sit quietly and fill out this mind map with the feelings, emotions, and words you feel right now. Having a mind map of your feelings will help you to get them out of your head, and you will be able to see them from a different perspective. What would you say if your friend was feeling depressed? Would you be angry with them, or would you be supportive?

Put yourself first, and don't worry about what others might think. You need to look after yourself. Be mindful of what your needs are. Try and communicate this to others so they understand what your needs are. Don't overreact to these feelings. They are just feelings. Be kind to yourself and listen to what your body and mind need right now.

TIPS FOR MANAGING DEPRESSION

Positive Self-Talk

Currently, in your life, with all the challenges you are facing, you need to self-soothe yourself and be your own best friend. Say things to yourself to make you feel better and let all the negative thoughts float away. They are not helping you at this moment in time; you are where you are, and that is okay. Accept where you are right now but also tell yourself that you are trying to figure it out and looking for new information to help you navigate your feelings. Positive self-talk is a great way to help you feel better and be more confident and stronger in your self-esteem to get through this challenging time.

Positive Psychology

The main aim of Positive Psychology is knowing yourself on a deeper level, which will help you feel more confident and positive about yourself. This will help you focus more on the positive aspects of yourself rather than the negative parts. By focusing on your negative parts, you are bringing a level of unease into your body which will trigger resentment and anger. You will begin to feel frustrated that you are not like other people, don't fit in, and are not normal.

However, uncovering the real you, your differences, and your strengths will help you to build a life of meaning and purpose. As a teenager, you may be feeling like you want to fit in with others and that you want to be normal. However, when you begin to understand that this is an impossibility, you can't be like your friend, you are *you*, then this brings you an inner strength that will help you control your feelings and emotions.

We all want you to flourish in your own way, and if you can communicate your needs to others, then it makes it easier for others to understand you better.

You may be feeling:

- People might not like me if they know the real me
- I might be rejected
- It will make me feel vulnerable

Those are the negative aspects of knowing yourself, but this is just fear – False Evidence Appearing Real! When you begin to understand yourself on a deeper level, you will begin to realize that you are a good person. You might have your own difficulties and quirkiness, but that makes you *YOU*. That is what makes you unique.

If you look at all the para-Olympian athletes, they are celebrating that they only have one arm or one leg. They are celebrating that this is who they are. You might not have any physical disabilities, but mental health must be seen this way too. Many famous people are now shouting out that they have ADHD or Dyslexia, which inspires other people.

Do you feel inspired when you watch these athletes? Do you think that maybe if they can do it, then you can too?

Finding your Strengths

This mindful exercise of finding your strengths may take time to uncover. Strengths are things that you are good at and come easily to you. They are unique to you. Start by making a mind map and put in the middle of the mind map 'Your Strengths.' If you don't know any yet, that is okay. Over time you will be able to add to this mind map.

Just start with one word or highlight the ones already on the mind map below. You don't need to be 100% certain because they change as you learn more about yourself. Put the mind map on your wall or anywhere you can see it daily.

What do you think your strengths are?

You might not be able to think positively about your strengths yet, but I invite you to pick one and put it on your mind map. If you have picked 'thoughtful,' then be mindful of how you apply this in your everyday life. You might think of other people or help your mum out when she is busy. You might be thoughtful when you buy a present for someone's birthday. You might just smile at someone who is having a hard day. There are many ways in which this strength will play out in your life.

Exercise

Pick a strength once a week and write down how you have applied this to your everyday life. This will help build your confidence and remember the positive side of being thoughtful. Don't forget these strengths also apply to YOU and not only to others. Do you bring thoughtfulness to yourself?

Finding your strengths will help you to flourish more in your life and live your best life. It is a simple exercise and will keep you feeling positive about yourself.

Gratitude Journal

What are you thankful for? Evidence shows that keeping a gratitude journal will increase your self-esteem and reduce stress. This is because, as above, you are focusing on the positive aspects of your life.

Do you focus on the negative part of your day or the positive?

If you are a pro at being negative, then changing your thoughts to being positive can be difficult. However, it will take time to re-train your mind to be positive. We are not taught this in schools, so if you can master this now while you are young, then the world is your oyster. Adults normally learn this in therapy when they have suffered a trauma, so you are already one step ahead of everyone else.

I can guarantee you that you will replay what went wrong in your day, like in a movie. You will think and think about it and make it bigger and bigger, probably bigger than the event. You can see how you can easily create a big story. Focusing on what went well in your day and being thankful no matter what happened will help you remain positive and retrain your mind.

Exercise

Find a special exercise book that you can keep by your bedside. I would keep a separate book/journal for this exercise. This is your gratitude journal.

Every night when you go to bed, write five positive things in your gratitude journal that went well in your day or what you are thankful for. It can be:

- Thank you for keeping my family safe
- Thank you for helping me to be mindful
- Thank you for the lovely dinner my mum cooked
- Thank you for the teachers that are trying to help me
- Thank you for reminding me to be positive
- Thank you for keeping me safe

What are you thankful for today?

- Thank you for ……….

Of course, you need to stay mindful in your day, so writing it down in your gratitude journal will also help you stay present and build up your muscle for being mindful.

When you are feeling negative and cannot think of anything to be thankful for, we all have days like this; you can read back what you wrote for the last day. Even copying what you wrote on a different day will help you get back into that positive mindset. This will help reduce your stress levels and make you happy.

Showing Gratitude

Now that you are mindful of what you are grateful for, it may be time to show that to others. This will also help you with your interpersonal skills with others.

How do you feel when others say, 'thank you for your help'? Does it make you feel happy?

I bet it does. However, you might not think the other person will also feel happy. Therefore, there are benefits for both of you. You will both feel happy, and it will probably make you smile. This will flood your body with the good feeling hormones and will make you feel happier and less stressed. Can you see how all these little techniques will add up to help you with your overall happiness?

Exercise

Once a week, tell someone that you are grateful for what they do for you or if someone has helped you. If you didn't say 'thank you' at the time, there is no reason why you can't say it on another day. Sometimes we are so busy and stressed that we don't recognize if someone is being kind or not. Maybe it is a daily thing so for instance, if your mum or dad cooks your dinner every day or makes sure you have lunch money, this is easily overlooked. How would you think your mum or dad would feel if you said, 'thank you for my lunch'? I would imagine that it would make them smile and feel good inside. It is indeed the little things that help.

Design your Perfect Day

It's time to get creative!

Imagery is a good way to trick your mind into being positive. As I said before, the mind doesn't know if it is real or imagined. That is why therapies like hypnotherapy and Neuro-Linguistic Programming work well because they can rewire the brain to make it feel positive rather than negative. Are you ready to do some trickery?

Exercise

Find a quiet place. Get a pen and paper and your journal. Take a deep breath and ask yourself what you would like your perfect day to be like. Draw or write words to describe your perfect day.

Here is what your perfect day might look like:

I wake up in a nice warm bedroom with all my favorite things around me. I walk down into the kitchen, and my mum is making me my favorite breakfast. I hug her and thank her for being so kind. She asks me what my day looks like, and I say that I don't know yet, so I will tell her after school. I walk to school, and the sun is shining, and I feel happy. I notice my feelings and do my mindfulness practice as I walk to school. I hear that the trees are rustling in the wind. I've never noticed that before. I hear the cars screaming past, and they don't bother me today. I feel positive and strong in who I am. I wave to my school friends at the gate, and they are all smiling at me. We walk to the classroom together. School was okay today, and I noticed how I felt in certain classes. My favorite teacher is Mrs. Harris because she is kind and caring. She helps me when I am struggling. I arrive home, and my mum hugs me again, and I tell her about my day. She is so happy that I am sharing my feelings. I feel happy that she is happy. I need my own space, so I say to my mum that I want to be alone, and she is happy. I go to my bedroom and shut everything out. It feels good to be on my own again.

I would advise that you do this exercise before you get out of bed and practice feeling happy in your body. You also need to bring color and feelings into this image. It is not just about the pictures and what you see; you must also use all your other senses. When you imagine your day, smile and maybe dance around your bedroom. Bring feelings of happiness and joy into the above image.

It doesn't matter if it doesn't happen or if you had a challenging day and felt out of control. That is okay. Everything you are feeling right now is okay. Practicing having a perfect day will retrain your brain from feeling negative to feeling positive. This will help you flourish in your life rather than just exist. Is this how you want to feel?

Every small step and technique you apply to your life will help in small ways.

All these techniques will help you to be positive about yourself, which will help you to manage your feelings healthily. Knowing yourself on a deeper level will benefit you in the long term, so keep practicing Positive Psychology.

I hope by reading this chapter on depression, you now feel more in control and able to identify when you are feeling low.

In Part 3, we will look at anger and ADHD.

Roundup

- Mindfulness – How are you feeling right now? How is it affecting your life? Journal or do mind maps to help you to understand what is happening.

- Emotional regulation – How do you want to feel? Do you feel happy or at peace? Pick one and imagine how you would feel if you were at peace. What could the feeling of depression teach you?

- Interpersonal effectiveness – Put your needs first. What do you need when you are feeling low? Get clarity on what you want and communicate that to others.

- Distress Tolerance – Don't fear your feelings of depression. It is just a feeling. Try and sit with this feeling, but do not judge or fall into what it might mean. Just be with the feeling. Breathe through this feeling.

PART III

COMPREHENSIVE DBT APPROACH: ANGER, ADHD

11

MANAGING ANGER IN NEURODIVERGENTS

Do you feel angry or aggressive? Do people frustrate you and make you angry?

Anger is just an emotion, and if you look back at the Feelings Wheel, you will see that you could be feeling many emotions. Here are a few of them:

Let down	Humiliated	Bitter	Mad	Aggressive
Frustrated	Distant	Critical	Betrayed	Resentful
Disrespected	Ridiculed	Furious	Jealous	Provoked
Hostile	Withdrawn	Number	Dismissive	Annoyed

As I mentioned, anger is perceived as a 'bad' emotion. However, anger can be seen as a good emotion if you healthily express this feeling.

Why Am I So Angry?

If you have been diagnosed with ADHD or Autism, then anger can be quite common. With both conditions, you may be unable to control your impulses and feelings, especially anger, and may find it difficult to calm yourself down.

You may feel like you fear anger more than the other emotions because others might say 'anger is bad' or that you simply can't express anger in a healthy way. You can, because like any other emotion and feeling, if you do not express it, it stays with your body and causes dis-ease. This chapter will teach you how to express anger healthily.

Anger can motivate you into action, but when you begin to feel that you are out of control and when you are harming yourself or others, you may need to seek help or try and manage yourself.

The good news is that it is manageable, and as we have seen in many of the chapters, it is a question of identifying what you are feeling, being mindful of how you are expressing them, and learning new techniques to help you feel in control.

What Does Anger Feel Like?

These are some of what you need to look out for:

- Sweaty palms
- Dizziness
- Shaking or trembling in the body
- Feeling hot, particularly in the neck and face
- Tense muscles
- Clenched jaw
- Tightness in your chest
- Increased heartbeat
- Weak in the legs
- Churning in your stomach

As you can see, you might feel one or two of them or very overwhelmed with how your physical body reacts when angry. Next time you feel angry, just check into your body with the mindfulness Body Scan Meditation in Chapter 9 to notice how your body reacts.

What Triggers Anger?

Anger can be triggered in several ways, and this feeling is just a part of how much you are feeling stressed. As I said before, if your bucket is full and somebody says something that makes you mad, this might trigger your anger. However, it doesn't mean that that person made you angry; it might be just that your bucket couldn't cope anymore, so it manifested into anger.

Can you see how managing your overall stress levels can help with the other emotions?

I remind you that:

It just doesn't fall out of the sky; there is always a build-up

Therefore, if you look at why you are feeling anger in the wider context, you will find that it will have other information for you. You might feel like you have taken on too much in that week and are anxious and worrying about school or socializing. Don't forget that having overwhelming emotions is a response to when you get to that breaking point. Keeping your levels of stress down helps you to be able to manage feelings of anger better. They won't be so strong.

Some of the triggers could be caused by:

- Stress
- Depression
- OCD
- ADHT
- A stage of grief

You may not realize that anger is a stage of grief, and if you are experiencing a loss in your close family, then feelings of anger are a normal part of the grieving process. If you are experiencing grief, talk to your parents, a close friend, or a teacher because they can help you make this trigger more manageable.

Why is Anger Bad?

The emotion isn't bad; it is how you react that might be perceived to be BAD. Anger is an issue if you are:

- Hurting others
- Impacting your relationships with others
- You are being verbally or physically abusive
- You worry and regret the things that you say
- You feel angry often
- You feel that your anger is out of control

If you feel your anger is out of control and harming you and others, it is time to see if you can change how you react to anger.

If anger is expressed in an unhealthy way, your parents might feel frightened as they might not know how to deal with you in this situation. Expressing anger in an unhealthy way can feel intimidating, so be mindful of how others might behave. You can help them to understand how you are feeling and what you need so they can help you and be comfortable around you.

To manage your anger, anger management techniques will help you to begin not to fear anger. You will feel confident that you will be able to identify and manage it healthily.

Expressing anger is a good thing, but you need to do it SAFELY. The following techniques will help you to manage anger more effectively.

Don't forget you can also apply your DBT techniques too.

DBT TECHNIQUES FOR ANGER

Mindfulness - Be Mindful and Not Mindless

Look at the Feelings Wheel again and see how you are feeling now. You may not identify it as anger. You may feel frustrated or irritated, or a situation might have triggered this feeling. Write down your feelings when you can and see in what situation you might have been triggered. This is all good information for you to be mindful of. Whenever that situation arises again, ask yourself these questions:

1. How would I like to manage it in the future?
2. What can I learn from this situation?

When you are mindless of your feelings and the triggers, you will feel helpless to change them. You may not be able to change them now, but you will learn from them. Everyone learns every day about their behaviors, their triggers, and themselves. This is a normal life process, and mindfulness will help you feel in control of your anger issues.

How Can I Change This Emotion?

Emotional regulation is about managing your feelings at the moment and in the future. Here is one of the DBT techniques, the STOP technique:

STOP = **S**top, **T**ake a Step Back, **O**bserve, **P**roceed Mindfully

When we are angry, sometimes we want to hurt others physically or by hurting someone's feelings. We want to lash out to try and express our emotions. DBT asks us to stop, take a step back, observe our feelings from a different place and think mindfully about how we can express anger or change the emotion to one that we feel is more appropriate in that situation.

What is the opposite emotion of anger?

Look at the Feelings Wheel and decide what emotion you want to feel when you are angry. Can you see what other emotions you can feel? Maybe you would like to feel thankful that you are feeling like this and that it has given you lots of information. A good one would be feeling inspired that you have experienced this emotion and acted well.

Positivity is the key to calming down your anger. Flood your body with some good-feeling hormones by smiling and dancing to music you love.

When you experience anger, it is difficult to feel anything other than bad about yourself; you can get pushed down into a rabbit hole where life is difficult, and you spiral down. This is known as being in victim mode and is a sticky place. By feeling positive, we can prevent this from happening. Seeing the good in everything will help you control these overwhelming feelings of anger, whether you perceive them to be bad or not.

When you are overrun with emotions, you may need to move. Moving your physical body will help you to maintain positivity, which is why dancing or exercising will help you change the state of your emotions.

Try it.

Exercise

I give you permission to feel SAD. Think of a time when you felt sad. Be mindful of how your body is reacting. Notice that your body may slump down. Your shoulders will fold onto your chest. Try and walk, and you will notice that maybe your feet are hard to pick up.

Now feel HAPPY. Think of a time when you felt happy. How is your body reacting? I bet it is standing up tall, your head is held high, and your feet are impatient to move. This feeling is excitement.

This is where you can trick your brain into thinking you are happy. When you are feeling angry, change your body position – stand up tall and smile, and the feelings of happiness will flood your body. It is not always about changing the feelings inside; you can change your physical body, too, to make yourself feel happy. Think about how you would like to move your body when feeling happy. Practice this so that when you are feeling angry, you can lift your head, put on some music, and dance. This will help you have a different feeling rather than anger.

How Can I Communicate This Feeling in a SAFE Way?

In the long-term, feeling good about yourself and having confidence are also important here. If you don't have any negative thoughts about yourself and the confidence that you have some techniques in your toolbox, you will feel in control to manage your anger. You will feel confident that you will be able to deal with whatever emotion you are feeling.

Communication is important in how you express yourself and how others perceive you. Interpersonal skills are also about how you communicate with yourself, not only with others. Therefore, whenever you are experiencing anger, do not give yourself a hard time.

Blaming Yourself

Negative self-talk will spiral you down into being a victim, and it will be difficult to change your emotions. This will increase your feelings of anger. Confidently speaking to yourself in a self-soothing way will help you to manage better.

Rather than saying:

> I've done it again. I'm angry with myself.
> Why can't I feel normal?
> Why does this always happen?
> It's all my fault.

Think more positively about yourself and affirm:

> I can handle this
> It is just a feeling
> I'm doing the best I can
> I love myself just the way I am

Listen out for 'It's all my fault' because this is such a common negative self-talk statement. Blaming yourself means you are in victim mode and, therefore, cannot change it.

Blaming Others

Maybe you are in a situation where others have triggered your anger. You may have felt frustrated that a person is not listening to you and that they ***made*** you angry. This is where building your interpersonal skills will help you communicate better, more confident about your feelings. Using the 'I' statement will help you effectively communicate emotion.

You can say:

> I feel angry about what you said
> I feel like you are blaming me

This takes away the conflict in the situation, and you will begin to feel more in control and calmer. You are taking ownership by saying, "I feel". Having good communication techniques in your toolbox will help you manage your anger healthily.

Distress Tolerance - How Can I Sit with these Feelings of Anger?

Sometimes it is not appropriate to change your feelings, and distress tolerance teaches us not to change these feelings of anger but to sit with them. Don't forget these emotions may have a message to tell you; therefore, taking time out to feel these emotions is a good thing. Journal anything that comes up. It is not easy sometimes because your automatic response is to run away or shout or scream. Therefore, how can you sit with these feelings of anger? One way is acceptance. Accept that this is just an emotion and self-soothe yourself.

Exercise

Positively speak to yourself. Remind yourself that:

> I am doing great.
> I am doing the best I can.

Sit in a quiet place and ask yourself what message does this feeling have? Journal whatever comes into your mind. Why not try talking to your anger and say:

Thank you for this feeling. What are you trying to tell me?

Acceptance is key to feeling less angry because you are not judging this emotion. It is just an emotion. Not good or bad. It is just so.

Write down whatever message it is trying to tell you. Perhaps you are not angry at all; maybe you are feeling frustrated, overtired, and stressed. Don't forget to look at the whole picture of your stress levels, physical health, and any worries that might be going on. Anger is only a small part of what you are experiencing right now. Using a mindful meditation will help you tune into your body for more answers to why anger has arisen. It could be something simple or complex, but either way, you have techniques and tools that will help you manage this better.

Not everyone is willing to look at their emotions, especially anger, so well done; it is a big step to listen to your emotions.

ANGER MANAGEMENT SKILLS FOR DIVERGENTS

You are now good at using your DBT techniques, but sometimes we need others to help us through this difficult emotion, which will help manage your stress and overwhelming emotions in the long term. Anger management techniques are a good short-term fix for those moments you feel like harming yourself or others.

Physically Expressing your Anger

When you have lots of adrenaline flooding your body, it will be difficult to calm down, and you will feel that you can't sit still for any length of time. That is when you need to express your anger – in a physically SAFE way.

You may express your anger in an UNSAFE way at the moment, and you can be mindful of this and learn to express it in a way that is safe for you and other people. Write down in what ways you are currently expressing your anger. Do you feel that this is the right action?

Remember that when you are angry, you will frighten people, and they will not know what to do. It is not that they are being unkind, they simply don't know how to deal with a person when they are physically abusive.

How to Express Your Anger Safely?

Below are seven ways in which you can healthily express your anger.

1. Move your body

Moving your body is a great way to release all your excessive adrenaline hormones. How can you move your body to release your anger? Do you want to walk? Do you want to dance? Do you just need to go out into nature and breathe? Be mindful of how your body wants to react to anger. Ask your body questions and be mindful of the answers. Your body will let you know what it needs in these moments if you listen.

2. Find a quiet space and be alone

Sometimes we just need time out, so if you recognize that you are angry, you may feel overwhelmed by people around you. Find a quiet space just to be and do your 7:11 breathing to calm yourself down. Or put on your headphones and find a relaxing guided meditation that will help you calm down. It is okay to find a quiet space but communicate this clearly to the people around you.

3. Beat a pillow

When you are feeling angry, it may be difficult to calm down, and your angry mind may want to hit out. Beating a pillow is a safe way to express your anger. Go to your bedroom and give a few punches to your pillow and release the anger inside you. This will help you to regain control of your anger.

4. Shout

Find a space where you won't frighten anyone and just SCREAM! Your body needs to express this anger, which is a great way of letting out a couple of screams. Does that feel good when you are angry? If your mum and dad are in the house, warn them that you feel like screaming. They might want to scream with you too.

5. Think before you speak

When we are overwhelmed by emotions, especially anger, we tend to say things that we will regret later. This can make you feel more frustrated and angrier in the long term. That is why it might be better to take time out to calm down and then think about it when you are calmer. If someone has made you angry, this is a good technique because you can just walk away and feel okay about that. You don't have to come up with a reply at the time, especially when you are feeling overwhelmed.

Take time out and calm down, and the situation will probably seem less traumatic than you thought when your angry feelings were overwhelming.

When you feel calmer, you can think about the right solution to handle the situation. Or you can ask for help and talk it through with someone. This all helps you to be aware of how you can manage your anger healthily.

6. Rest and exercise

The key to managing your overall stress levels is to get as much rest and exercise as you feel necessary. Rest is important because you will be able to feel calmer. Especially if you are sleeping because your bucket is empty, and you can begin your next day in a much better place. Even if you must take a nap in the afternoon, when you can, that is okay. Listen to your body and see what it needs. Does it need to rest? Does it need to exercise? This is a good exercise to be mindful of how your body feels.

7. Communicate clearly

You may feel unable to communicate to others how you are feeling at the moment, but you can when the anger has passed. If you had to walk away from a conversation or a potentially triggering event, then you can always try and explain what happened. Communicating with someone about your needs will help others understand what is going on in your head.

Unlike a physical disability, people cannot see what is going on; only you know the day-to-day challenges that you mentally face. Communicating clearly will help you not feel bad about your outbursts of anger and any overwhelming emotion. Help people understand what is going on for you, and they will be able to help you back. Find a style of communication that works well for you whether it is by text, a letter, a phone call, or an email. In the 21st century, it doesn't have to be face-to-face if you find this challenging. Find something that works for you.

As you can see, there are lots of techniques that will help you manage your stress healthily. Anger is a natural emotion, so do not beat yourself up about feeling angry or frustrated. It is a normal feeling, and you will be surprised at how many people feel angry every day. You might want to ask them.

Expressing emotions is healthy but in a safe way that doesn't harm you or anyone else. Remember that and don't try and hang onto the emotion of anger.

If you suffer from ADHD, then the next chapter is for you. This can be a challenging mental health condition, but this will help you to identify and accept your mental health condition.

Roundup

- Mindfulness – be mindful of situations that can trigger your anger. Use imagery to trick your mind into feeling positive.

- Emotional regulation – Identify what you feel in the moment using the Feelings Wheel. See if you change the feeling by using the techniques that work for you.

- Interpersonal effectiveness – communicate how you feel in the moment or when you are calmer. Be kind to yourself and say positive things.

- Distress Tolerance – find a quiet place and express your emotions in a SAFE way. Be with your anger and see what information it is trying to tell you.

12

MANAGING ADHD IN NEURODIVERGENTS

In Chapter 2, you learned about neurodivergent people and how differently their brain works. Neurodivergent people may also have mental health conditions like ADHD or Autism.

You may have been diagnosed with ADHD (Attention Deficit Hyperactivity Disorder), which contributes to high stress levels and behavioral problems. Throughout this book, I have included exercises to help with this condition. However, in this chapter, we will specifically look at ADHD.

WHAT IS ADHD?

ADHD will affect your behavior, so the techniques you have learned so far may be a little challenging, but they are still manageable. You may need to adjust the exercises to suit you.

If you know you are restless and find it difficult to sit still, you may have to adapt to whatever your condition allows you. If sleeping is an issue for you, then you might find the bedtime routine helpful that we spoke about in Chapter 9. There are ways in which you can manage ADHD and how it affects you, but sometimes you might need medication and support from a health professional.

The first step is to become aware of your condition and be mindful of how this condition impacts your life. You might have to talk it through with a professional or your parents, but that is okay. If you can't manage it yourself, then ask for support.

ADHD is often diagnosed under 12 years old but can be diagnosed in adults too and normally improves with age. However, it can go undetected, which can be frustrating. You are not a naughty child; your brain is functioning differently and educating those around you will help them understand your condition.

You may find it difficult to self-control your emotions, but again, the techniques in this book will guide you through this difficulty. Be gentle with yourself and understand that it might take you a little longer because of the challenges you have with ADHD but find the right strategies that work well for you.

What Are the Symptoms of ADHD?

If you are suffering from ADHD, then these are the things that you might find difficult:

- Being organized
- Impulsive behavior
- Sleeping at night
- Shopping
- Listening to instructions
- Time management
- Coping with stress
- Unable to concentrate

ADHD, Depression, and Anxiety, do they Coexist?

ADHD can be challenging, and 80% of people with ADHD will also have depression or anxiety. It could be a result of living with ADHD and your challenges. If you are on medication for ADHD, then this can result in anxiety.

ADHD, depression, and anxiety frequently occur together, as ADHD can trigger anxiety and depression. If your stress bucket is overflowing with all the challenges and struggles you are facing with your ADHD, you might struggle to empty your bucket, which will then cause anxiety or depression. For your body to cope with the overwhelm you are facing, lowering your overall stress levels will help. Don't forget ADHD is already taking up a lot of your brain time with you unable to focus, so be kind to yourself and learn some strategies to deal with ADHD and all its challenges.

Types of ADHD

There are three types of ADHD:

1. Inattentive Type ADHD

The signs of the Inattentive Type are lack of attention and distractibility. There are no signs of hyperactive behavior. People with this type have weak working memories and frequently lose things. They always make mistakes, fail to pay attention and keep on task. They frequently do not listen and are unable to follow or understand instructions.

2. Hyperactive-Impulsive Type ADHD

The signs are hyperactivity and impulsive behavior. They lack self-control. They will fidget and squirm and be unable to sit still. They will run or climb at inappropriate times and talk too much. They will have trouble playing quietly.

3. Combined Type ADHD

This is a mix of both hyperactive-impulsive behaviors and inattention-distracted behavior.

All the exercises and information in this book will help any type. Be aware of what type you might be and be mindful of what symptoms you are presenting to manage your ADHD effectively. If you can't sit still, then exercise or walking meditations will help you. If you find it difficult to remember things, then journaling or writing down things will help. The following tips and exercises will help you to navigate your ADHD.

How to Manage Sensory Overload Effectively?

People suffering from ADHD and Autism are likely to experience sensory overload, which you might have a challenge with.

Do you feel like your head is going to explode from loud noises?

Do big crowds and parties with noisy music overwhelm you?

When you are in those situations you may:

- Lose focus on what is happening around you
- Become restless
- Become irritated
- Become overwhelmed
- Feel your stress levels increase
- Feel like you want to cover your eyes and ears
- Feel like you want to avoid or run away from these situations

Sensory overload is when your brain cannot interpret competing for sensory information. Your brain cannot filter out all the noises; therefore, the brain becomes confused and sends panic signals to the body. This reaction will leave you feeling panicked and wanting to run away.

There may be certain situations where you feel unable to cope, so it is a good idea to be mindful of those situations. Do not try and avoid them because it will send a message to the brain that these places are a threat, and every time you go into that situation, the brain will remember and turn on the panic mode. What would be more useful is that you have some coping strategies to deal with these overloads.

Exercise

Journal these situations; did they have bright lights or lots of unfamiliar people? Was it new? How did you feel? How did you cope with it? Fill out the table below so you have the information about how you felt and what the situation was. This will be helpful to show your parents so they understand what went wrong and how you can all manage the same situation better.

Below is an example:

Date	What was the situation?	What was the sensory overload?	How did I feel?	How did I cope with it?	What did I learn from that situation?
29.11.22	Supermarket	Bright lights, many people, loud noises, unfamiliar bangs	Scared and angry. I wanted to run away.	I went outside to breathe.	That I need to go to the supermarket when it isn't so busy.

Breathe

An effective way to manage your feelings in these situations is to simply breathe. Do your 7:11 breathing, breathe in for 7 and out for 11. You might want to go outside to do this, and this is okay. Tell the person that you are with that you need to go outside. Find a quiet place to sit and close your eyes. This will block out any of the sensory challenges you might be facing. Cover your ears and close your eyes if you want to block out everything. Just be with yourself, breathe and tune into your body. Try not to let your emotions overwhelm you, breathe until you feel calmer.

USING DBT PRINCIPLES TO MANAGE ADHD

Let's recap the four pillars of DBT and how they will help people suffering from ADHD. There are also some tips on living with ADHD and exercises to help you feel more in control.

Mindfulness

If you are not mindful of how ADHD affects your life and behavior, then you cannot change it. Mindfulness will help you identify how this condition affects you without judgment. It will teach you to be mindful in the present moment, which will reduce your overall anxiety, and you will begin to build up strategies that will help you not to overreact to a situation. You will mainly focus on what is happening in the here and now and not worrying about the past or the future. You will begin to calm down the restlessness by reducing your overall stress levels.

The more mindful you are, the more you will recognize the behavioral and thinking patterns you are running. This will build up your confidence and self-esteem, which will help with your condition.

The message throughout this book is that there isn't one strategy or technique that will help you; it will be a combination of things that will improve your life. Being mindful is the first step to being aware so that you can change.

Exercise

How does ADHD affect your life?

Again, let's do a mind map:

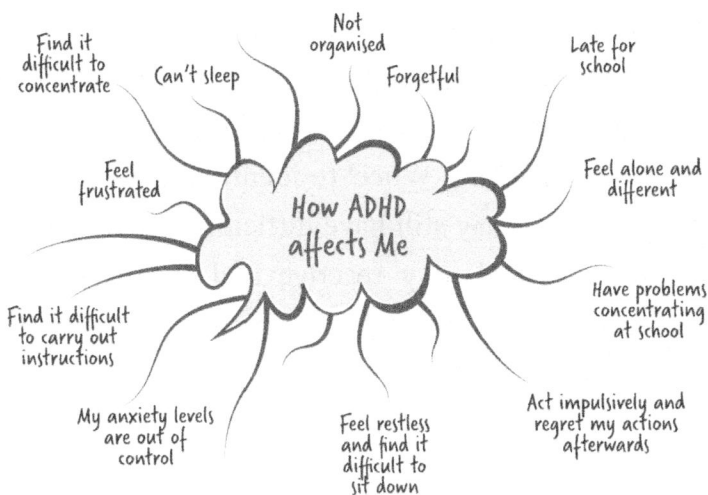

Add the symptoms that you are experiencing in the empty strands. Do not judge your symptoms or feelings or feel low about your condition. You are not trying to change anything at this stage. You are being mindful of how it affects your life. Once you are armed with this information, you will feel more in control of how to use the strategies in this book.

You can use colors to represent what things are the most difficult. For example, if you find feeling lonely is your main challenge, then put that word in red. When you are ready, sharing this with your parents and therapists trying to help you will be useful. They will be so surprised that you are being proactive with your condition. You may feel like you want to be independent now that you are an adolescent; this is a good first step to taking control of your condition.

Emotional Regulation

It can be exhausting when you have overwhelming emotions you are trying to control, so this strategy teaches you how to identify your feelings but not act on them. You have learned how to use the Feelings Wheel to identify them, so you are a pro now, but you may still have difficulties in not acting on them. You may feel very reactive and impulsive to your emotions, so let's create some strategies for you with that.

Exercise

Keep a diary of how certain emotions make you act and what were the circumstances. The below example will help you.

What was the emotion?	How did I feel I wanted to react?	What situation was I in?	How can I react differently?
Anger	I wanted to hurt someone.	School was annoying	I can have accepted anger as anger and taken some time out

Writing down your emotions and how you reacted doesn't make them right or wrong. It helps you identify where you might want to change that emotion. Again, do not judge how you have reacted at this stage; we need the information so you can change it. In certain situations, anger is acceptable but not if it harms you or others, physically or emotionally. This will make you feel more regretful in the future and increase your stress levels.

Identifying where you might have shown an emotion differently will help to retrain your brain so that in the same situation, you can react differently. Learning new strategies and techniques takes time, so be kind to yourself. You are doing something different in recognizing where you could have done better, which takes courage and strength.

Interpersonal Effectiveness

DBT works for ADHD because it focuses on social and emotional challenges in your life. This helps you change for the better and having great social and personal skills will help you have a deeper understanding of who you are. ADHD people find socializing difficult, and you may find being in public spaces difficult because of the noise. Learning how to become more sociable is a good thing, and also learning some coping strategies so that you do not have to worry about social settings will reduce your overall stress levels.

If you have completed all the exercises throughout this book, then you will be armed with enough information about yourself and your condition that you can use to communicate with others. You can either show your parents or teachers your mind maps or your diary entries so they can understand your challenges. However, if you feel these are too personal, pick one you are comfortable with to show them.

For example, if you find playing sports with others challenging, you can say to your teacher:

"When I play sports, I feel overwhelmed and frustrated. The noise makes my head hurt, and that is why I get angry."

Don't forget to use the 'I' statement.

The teacher will respect you for that because it takes courage to speak out about your condition but also, she will be able to adapt the situation to meet your needs so that you can feel comfortable and not worry about playing sports at school. This will help with your overall stress, and by now, you will know that it helps this condition immensely.

Worrying about things increases your stress levels, which in turn will make your symptoms of ADHD worse. Therefore, reducing your overall stress regarding things you worry about will be very useful. Communicating that to your family and teachers will help you in the long run. Don't be scared to speak out. You are having a very challenging time at the moment and you may feel frustrated. Speaking out will help others to understand and for you to feel more comfortable.

Don't forget you cannot control what others think about you (look at the Control Wheel in Chapter 6) so speaking out about your challenges is a healthy way of expressing your feelings and emotions.

The DEAR MAN DBT technique will also be helpful because it outlines a strategy for expressing your wants and needs.

Describe – Clearly describe the facts of the situation.

Express – Using "I" statement.

Assert – Be specific about what you want or need.

Reinforce – Say thank you if the person responds well to you.

Mindfulness – Be mindful of your goals, so you are not distracted.

Appear Confident – Stand up straight, make eye contact, and speak clearly.

Negotiate – Know what you are willing to accept. Know your boundaries.

You can find the worksheet at

https://www.therapistaid.com/worksheets/dbt-dear-man,

Interpersonal skills are not all about communicating with other people, they are also based on you and what kind of relationship you have with yourself.

How Do You Feel About Yourself?

It is important to feel good about yourself, be kind, and only say positive things to yourself. This will help self-soothe you when you are focusing on challenges. Confidence is also an important thing to consider. The more challenges you face, the more you will begin to trust that you can cope, increasing your confidence. When you are first diagnosed as having ADHD, you might feel like you don't like yourself at all.

Love yourself just the way you are

We all have flaws and face challenges in our lives, as well as strengths and weaknesses. Being okay with them and radically accepting that this is where you are in your life will help you to find your strengths. Finding your strengths will give you confidence that you are good at some things and can use these in your everyday life rather than focusing on your flaws.

These strengths can be:

- Energetic and fun
- Great problem solver
- Sensitive to others and more compassionate
- Creative
- Great imagination
- Great sense of humor
- You can achieve the impossible
- Great sense of observation
- You thrive on multitasking
- You have super-focus
- Strong moral compass – what is right and wrong

You can also look at these positive strengths as your superpowers.

WHAT ARE YOUR SUPER-POWERS?

Rather than looking at the negative effects of having ADHD, there are so many positives. These can be called your superpowers.

Exercise

Write down your superpowers or draw a picture with you in the middle with a super cape on like Batman. Sit quietly and imagine how you would use your superpowers. Be super creative with your drawing to recreate that image in your mind.

Bring some feeling into this picture. How do you feel? Strong, confident, funny, inspired? Imagining your superpowers and adding feelings to this picture will help you to feel more positive rather than negative about your condition and install new patterns.

You may find other things a little challenging, but you have more fun with your superpowers.

Use your superpowers wisely.

Distress Tolerance

This is all about how to learn to sit with your painful emotions and situations that seem overwhelming and to avoid behavior that makes things worse. Having overwhelming emotions about your condition can make you act the wrong way for yourself and others. Teenagers with

ADHD typically have outbursts of emotions and this is where you need to be mindful to take the right action. By thinking about these outbursts of emotions logically and calming down the emotions you will begin to have a different perspective. Emotions can overtake your logical brain; therefore, sitting with these feelings will help you put them into context.

Your emotions can seem like they are running the show, and you cannot help them. Of course, you can; you just need to have the right techniques we have discussed throughout this book. The best course of action is to practice Radical Acceptance. This is a great DBT technique to practice in these situations.

Remember: the key to transformation is acceptance.

Radical Acceptance

Radical acceptance will help accept the undesirable situation and the fact that you have ADHD. Sometimes you cannot change the circumstances and what triggers your emotions, so the next step is to accept your condition and feel at peace. Accept that you may have to deal with difficult and challenging emotions. You need to radically accept this, making you feel calmer and in control.

You may not want to accept these feelings or that you have been diagnosed with ADHD, but it will lower your stress levels if you do.

When you are feeling overwhelmed with life and your condition, you have a choice. You can be sad about it, frustrated, or even angry. You don't accept the situation and blame everyone else. Or, you have a choice to say, "Okay, let's get on with it."

Don't worry because radical acceptance is not all about accepting that it will never change. It will change, and you will feel in control again, but at this moment, you have ADHD.

Ask yourself these questions:

Do you accept that you have ADHD?

Do you accept that you can be at peace with this?

Do you accept that you can feel in control of this condition?

Journal the answers to these questions and see how you feel about ADHD and how you think you can start living with it.

By accepting this part of you, you will begin to look at the positives of what this condition will bring you and not look at it so negatively. When you have chosen to accept it, you can then change.

Imagine that you fear going to the dentist. You have ignored it and not accepted that you are scared. You have a bad toothache and you keep not accepting that this is hurting you. You avoid going to the dentist by negatively projecting that you won't be able to cope, that you will have an emotional outburst and that people will point their finger at you. You are also scared of all the instruments the dentist uses. You are negatively focusing by saying; What if? What if I don't like it? What if I can't leave? What if …

By avoiding the dentist, you then begin to manage the pain. You don't eat cold foods and try to ignore that you have a bad tooth. You have been told that sugar is bad for your teeth, so you avoid those foods too. The bad tooth is beginning to get worse, and nothing works. The pain is increasing every minute.

By practicing radical acceptance, you choose to accept that you fear going to the dentist. This is a courageous thing to do. You talk to your parents about it, and they come up with a solution of maybe going to talk to the dentist before you have the treatment. However, you have accepted where you are right now, and you begin to feel better.

Try some of these techniques to help you with accepting you have ADHD.

Self-soothe

Be kind to yourself. Pat yourself on the back for reading this book to help you understand more about your condition and learn new techniques. Tell yourself:

I am doing great.

I am proud of myself for handling this condition.

Say these words out loud. How do they feel? Is it better than thinking negatively about yourself?

Talking positively to yourself is a great thing to do. It affirms that you are a good person despite your challenges. Focus on the fact that you are doing your best, which is okay. You are learning about yourself every day, and that is a good thing.

You can also do something physical to self-soothe. Do something that you love to do. Write, draw, or go for a walk. Be mindful of your needs and if you need quiet time, then communicate this, or if you need to be around people, then do that. You have choices in how you self-soothe yourself. It may be that you want your favorite ice cream, which will make you happy. Do things to self-soothe that make YOU happy. Be mindful of what things you do to self-soothe.

Accept Yourself and Your Limitations

We all have limitations in our lives, whether we can see them or not. I guarantee you that if you do a survey and ask others how they were feeling, you will begin to see that you are not the only one suffering from mental health limitations. Accept yourself for who you are and what challenges you are facing. You may have bigger limitations than others, but that is okay.

Radically accept you and your limitations. It is okay, and you are doing a great job. Celebrate this acceptance, dance around your bedroom, and whoop whoop. I bet that made you feel better.

I hope this chapter has taught you that whatever mental health condition you have, you can help yourself manage this condition. You just need to accept and be mindful of how ADHD affects your life and what strategies work well for you.

Don't be frightened that this condition will ruin your life and that there is nothing you can do about it. There is something you can do about it, and I hope this chapter has helped you to manage your ADHD better.

In the next chapter, you will learn about everything you need to know to keep a healthy mind and body.

> **Roundup**
>
> - Mindfulness – Be mindful of how this condition affects your daily life.
>
> - Emotional regulation – How do your emotions make you react? Try to keep a diary of how certain emotions make you feel and how you react to them. Learn different strategies to act differently.
>
> - Interpersonal effectiveness – communicate your condition to others to help them understand why you might find life challenging. Learn to raise your self-esteem and self-soothe your worries.
>
> - Distress Tolerance – can you accept that you may have emotional outbursts? Radical acceptance is the key to accepting your condition and where you are in your life right now.

OVERVIEW: EVERYTHING YOU NEED TO KNOW TO KEEP A HEALTHY MIND AND BODY

Throughout this book, we have looked at certain conditions and how to apply DBT techniques to social anxiety, stress, depression, and anger. We also looked at ADHD and how neurodivergent people (whose brains function differently) can manage these symptoms. The common factor in managing neurodivergence and ADHD is to look after your overall stress levels. Therefore, in this chapter, we will recap how to manage your overall health, mind, and body so that you can live a more mindful and stabilized life.

If you are constantly stressed, your body reacts to this, leaving you feeling more emotional and out of control. It will also create panic in your body, and you will continually feel nervous.

Your mind and body are already struggling if you have a mental health condition; therefore, looking at your overall health will be beneficial. As I said before, it is not a quick fix, you need to practice long-term strategies to help you through this difficult period. If you want to build muscles, you can't just go to the gym a couple of times. It takes time to build your muscles; this is the same for your physical and mental health and well-being.

This chapter might also be helpful if you would like to share the information with your parents. You can educate them that you need to keep overall wellness, and it is not just about managing your condition.

We generally take care of our physical health but then ignore our mental health until it becomes a problem. You need to learn how to keep your body and mind fit and healthy to live the life you want.

TOP 10 TIPS FOR LIVING A MINDFUL AND MORE EMOTIONALLY STABLE LIFE

Throughout this book, we have talked about how to manage your mental and emotional health, and here are ten top tips to keep you in balance.

1. Keeping physically healthy

This is a great way to keep active and turn your mind off. If you do any exercise you love, your body is flooded with the good feeling hormone. It will also help to reduce the amount of adrenalin in your body. Keeping active helps your mental state and keeps your heart and physical body healthy. I find when I exercise that all my self-talk in my head quietens down as I am physically focusing on doing the exercise. You may find this helps to quieten down your worries too.

Do an activity that you love and try and schedule it twice a week. Don't forget, being mindful when you are doing the activity will help you keep focused. Journal afterward how you felt when you exercised. This will help you keep motivated.

2. Eat Healthily

Eating healthily also plays a part in keeping your physical body healthy. Watch out for sugary foods and foods with additives. Eat more fresh vegetables and fruit, which are all good for you and help your body balance.

3. Be Kind to Yourself

When you are unkind to yourself, it will be difficult to change as you will continually beat yourself up all the time. Think of yourself as your new best friend. What would you say to your best friend in these challenging times? What wouldn't you say?

Unkind words can be damaging when you say them out loud to others and when you say them to yourself, even if they are just thoughts. This will keep you in the stress cycle and lower your self-esteem. If you can't feel good about yourself, you cannot change your life. If you like or love yourself, then you will treat yourself kinder. You can be kind to your physical body, like eating healthily and exercising, but we forget to be kind to our thoughts and emotions and accept how we are feeling rather than dismissing it.

Be mindful when you are being unkind to yourself and STOP. Stop to think about how this is damaging your overall health and what other thoughts and feelings you can have to show yourself that you care about *yourself*.

4. Spend time with people you enjoy

If you feel lonely or frustrated about your mental health condition, being around people you enjoy will help you keep positive. When you are alone, you generally think more negatively about your mental health. Sometimes thoughts will keep going round and round in circles. Sometimes you need to take a break from this negative thinking and being around others will help you to focus on something different.

Being around people you have fun with is less stressful than going into challenging social situations. Let yourself off the hook for a night and have fun with the people you love.

5. Pursue a new hobby / new activity

Sometimes we can get stuck in everyday living, and we get bored. If you are bored, you are likely to feel frustrated and maybe even angry. Finding a new hobby or activity will refocus your mind on something different. If you do the same thing, you get the same results, and thereby introducing a new interest will inspire you and make you feel happier.

Have you ever wanted to learn how to play the guitar? Do you want to learn how to paint? Do you want to learn more about computers?

This is all possible if you manage your time well and make space for this new hobby or activity.

Doing what you love also helps to lower your stress levels and keeps you focused away from your thoughts and worries.

6. Practice gratitude

By now, you will have a separate journal in which you have written down five things you are grateful for every day. Keep this up, and maybe write down ten things you are grateful for every day. By practicing gratitude, you will begin to feel more positive about yourself and your situation. Dwelling on negative things doesn't help and will add to your stress levels. By feeling more positive you will feel more able to cope with your emotions and feelings and feel in control of any situation.

7. Meditation

I would recommend regularly using guided meditations. You can also use mindfulness meditations to help you to stay present. Don't worry if you can't sit still throughout the whole meditation; maybe try walking meditation with your headphones on. This has the same effect. So, find a way that works for you.

This will help you calm your mind down and lower your stress levels. There are plenty of apps with guided meditations that will help. Try out Insight Timer or Calm.

8. Mindfulness Techniques

You have learned many mindfulness techniques throughout this book. Look back at the techniques that you enjoyed the most. Make a list of them so you know how to use them and what works for you. You will feel confident and more in control when you are armed with the right techniques.

9. Express yourself in a healthy way

Practicing your interpersonal skills will help you to express your feelings and emotions healthily. We have talked a lot about these techniques but remember the most important relationship is the one you have with yourself. If you know how you are feeling and what others can do to help you, you will better communicate this. It is difficult to communicate and express yourself when you don't know what your needs are.

Being self-assured and confident is a must when you are expressing your needs. Stand tall and say what you want in the most effective way. You can use the 'I' statement. I felt fear when you said that. Using this technique, there is no blame on you or the other person. Your feelings cannot be wrong if you express them this way. It is when you start blaming the other person. For example, if you say, "you **made** me feel fearful."

Do you notice the difference? How would you react if someone said, "you **made** me"? You might feel angry and resentful, which isn't helpful for you to regulate your emotions.

To be healthy in expressing your emotions, always use the 'I' statement.

10. Ask for help

Don't suffer alone. There is no shame in having a mental health condition, and you must speak out. Be brave and say, "This is me," and people around you will be able to help and understand you more. Know what your needs and wants are and what help you need. Be mindful that some things you won't be able to do on your own or understand, and it is okay to ask for help from others. Be open and vulnerable, and people will begin to see the real you.

Roundup

- Mindfulness – Practice mindfulness every day. Try the body scan to check in with your emotions. Try Insight Timer or Calm to find new mindfulness meditations.

- Emotional regulation – Identify your emotional needs. Practice being more emotionally intelligent.

- Interpersonal effectiveness – Use the 'I' statement to communicate your feelings effectively. Don't blame yourself or others; this is just how you feel, and it is no one's fault.

- Distress Tolerance – Be okay to sit with uncomfortable feelings. Feelings are just feelings. Do not judge. Radical acceptance is the key to transformation.

CONCLUSION

Do you know more about your neurodivergent condition?

Do you know more about yourself?

In Chapter 1, you drew a mind map of how you felt at the beginning of the book. Go back and look at it now and see if these feelings have changed. Re-draw the mind map. Is it any different?

How are you feeling now?

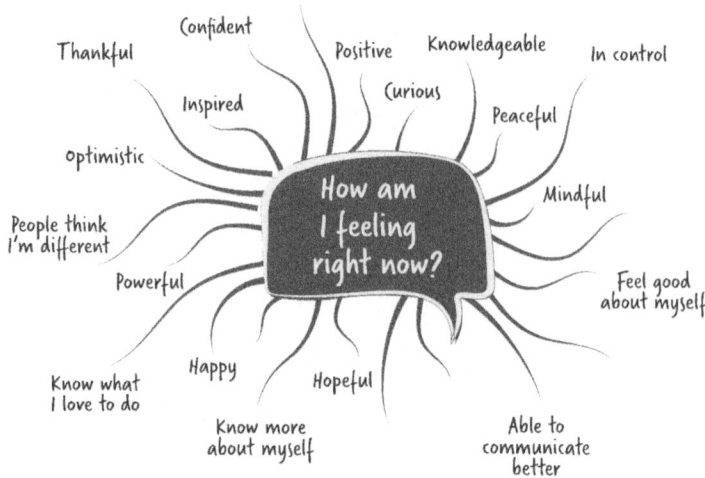

Feel free to add any of your words in the empty strands of how you feel. Some of them might still not be positive, but that's okay. Honor how you are feeling right now. You may feel excited, in control, and have more knowledge of your condition, but most of all, I hope that you feel more confident to move forward in your life positively.

The hope is that by reading this book and carrying out the exercises, you feel confident to manage your condition and unlock your highest potential. You deserve to live the best life possible, and it is possible! I won't lie to you that your condition is challenging, but the good news is that it can be managed. If you have the determination and the right information, you can better manage where you are right now.

I want you to feel that you are 'normal', whatever that means, and that you do not feel isolated and an outcast. Adolescence can seem very confusing, but you will come out on the other side with more information about yourself.

Learning about yourself is a lifelong process, and you will evolve as a human being. That is what makes us so unique and apart from other species because we can choose to change.

There is a saying that if you always do the same thing, you will get the same results, which is why it is not just about reading this book. You need to take action and do the exercises. Find a few exercises and DBT techniques that you feel help you the best and stick with them. If they are not working, change them. It is not a failure on your part, one exercise may work for a while, and then it might not. As you evolve and change, so may the techniques, so be mindful when you need to change it up a bit.

You may find communicating with others still challenging, but please stick with this because it is a life skill worth gaining confidence in. Social skills will help you not only in the future but also to communicate how you are feeling and will help you manage your condition.

At the start of this book, you may have been feeling frustrated that you were diagnosed with a neurodivergent condition, and I hope that by the time you are reading this that this has changed.

Be mindful of the journey you have taken by reading this book. Share the techniques with your family and friends and educate them about your condition. Don't hide and be shameful. It is where you are at the moment, so embrace that part of you. It may last only for a short while, but that is okay. You can manage your condition, and you can change.

Your condition may also have induced anxiety and depression but take comfort in that all human beings are affected by both these conditions, so it is not just you. We all have to manage our mental health, and it is only when it fails us that we take notice. How many people have the condition that you have and are not willing to do anything about it? You are, you have made a great step in picking up this book, learning about your condition, and taking steps to change. It takes courage, and not everyone can do that. Pat yourself on the back.

Take a deep breath, relax your shoulders, and tell yourself:

I am courageous.

I am proud of myself

As you know by now, positivity and self-talk are the most important things to master. I hope that one day it will be taught in schools to young children because it is needed in this social media society.

Social media tells us what is normal and what is not, bringing added pressure onto young people today. However, what I have learned is that being yourself, and being unique, will help your future self to be successful. By accepting who you are, your strengths and flaws, other people will appreciate the honesty and rawness that you will bring.

Don't forget the opening of the book:

"Be you, everyone else is taken"

— OSCAR WILDE

Our emotions and feelings can take us down a spiral pathway, and it too may be extra challenging to try and control these emotions. The exercises in this book will help you, but I would suggest the one thing to master is mindfulness. This will be the key to being aware of what message your emotions and feelings are trying to tell you, but also, you will feel in control. Expressing emotions is a must and one you must do safely and healthily for yourself and others. Put the Feelings Wheel somewhere you can see it every day and remind yourself that feelings are just feelings and you will be able to cope no matter what. Being positive about where you are will also help, so practice smiling, standing tall, and thinking good things about yourself.

The biggest obstacle will be learning about yourself to be more self-sufficient with your emotions and mental health condition. Don't hand over control of how you feel; you need to find ways to express them healthily.

Whatever you want to do in life, you can do it. It is about being aware of what you want and how, with your mental health condition and your superpowers, you can achieve this. This is a journey of self-discovery and awareness, and I am hopeful that this book has brought this all to light.

I am excited for you to continue your journey. If you need any further information or techniques, you can find these in the Further Information section.

What Does Your Future Look Like?

Now that you are feeling better, take a moment to imagine your future. Get excited that you can live the life you want. Answer the questions below and begin to imagine what your future could look like.

Exercise

Ask yourself these questions:

1. What are your deepest desires?
2. What do you dream about being or doing?
3. What do you want to achieve in your life?
4. What is holding you back?

Draw a picture or a mind map or write in your journal the answers to the above questions. If you don't know where you want to go, you will not arrive at your destination, so this is a great exercise to finish with. Keep this safe, and whenever you feel stressed, depressed, or angry, then these answers will keep you motivated and on track.

Whatever your dreams and desires, feel confident and self-assured that you can achieve these.

Lastly, in Johnny Depp's words:

> *I think everybody's weird. We should all celebrate our individuality and not be embarrassed or ashamed of it.*
>
> — JOHNNY DEPP

USEFUL INFORMATION SECTION AND FURTHER TOOLS

DBT Skills for Emotional Regulation - https://dbt.tools/emotional_regulation/index.php

DBT Workbooks - https://www.therapistaid.com/therapy-worksheets/communication/adolescents

DBT Workbook (Dear Man) – https://www.therapistaid.com/worksheets/dbt-dear-man

Distress Tolerance - https://depts.washington.edu/uwbrtc/about-us/dialectical-behavior-therapy/#:~:text=Components%20of%20DBT

DBT Therapist for Group Therapy - https://www.betterhelp.com/ca/

Dialectical Behavior Therapy - https://depts.washington.edu/uwbrtc/about-us/dialectical-behavior-therapy/#:~:text=Components%20of%20DBT

Free Guided Meditations https://www.rbht.nhs.uk/our-services/clinical_support/rehabilitation-and-therapies/psychological-medicine/relaxation-exercises

Learn more about Judy Singer - http://www.myspectrumsuite.com/meet-judy-singer/

National Institute of Mental Health - https://www.nimh.nih.gov/

Neurodivergent - https://www.verywellhealth.com/neurodivergent-5216749

Psychwire - https://psychwire.com/profiles/cv4k3l/marsha-linehan

Understanding your emotions - https://www.verywellmind.com/the-purpose-of-emotions-2795181

Wellmind - https://www.verywellmind.com/

World Health Organization – Adolescent Mental Health - https://www.who.int/news-room/fact-sheets/detail/adolescent-mental-health

RESOURCES

5 Most Common Mental Disorders - https://www.dbhutah.org/the-5-most-common-mental-disorders/ *[2022]*

7 Myths About Mental Health - https://www.unicef.org/parenting/health/busted-7-myths-about-mental-health *[Unicef 2022]*

7/11 Breathing Technique - https://www.hgi.org.uk/resources/delve-our-extensive-library/resources-and-techniques/7-11-breathing-how-does-deep *[Human Givens Blog 2012]*

Anger - https://www.verywellmind.com/why-am-i-always-angry-5184554 *[Fuller 2022]*

Anger Manager - https://www.mayoclinic.org/healthy-lifestyle/adult-health/in-depth/anger-management/art-20045434 *[Mayo Clinic Staff 2022]*

ADHD - https://www.cdc.gov/ncbddd/adhd/facts.html *[2022]*

Autism & ADHD - https://www.verywellhealth.com/autism-vs-adhd-5213000 *[Rudy & Gans 2022]*

ADHD - https://www.nhs.uk/conditions/attention-deficit-hyperactivity-disorder-adhd/symptoms/ *[2021]*

Coping with Social Anxiety - https://www.verywellmind.com/coping-with-social-anxiety-disorder-3024836 *[Cuncic 2021]*

Dialectical Behavioral Therapy - https://www.webmd.com/mental-health/dialectical-behavioral-therapy#:~:text=Dialectical%20behavioral%20therapy%20(DBT)%20is *[Taylor 2022]*

Depression - https://www.nimh.nih.gov/health/topics/depression *[2022]*

Depression - https://www.medicalnewstoday.com/articles/8933 *[2022]*

Emotional Regulation - https://www.betterup.com/blog/emotional-regulation-skills?hs_amp=true *[Klynn 2021]*

How to Manage Sensory Overload - https://www.sensoryfriendly.net/how-to-manage-sensory-overload-in-adults/ [Cooke 2021]

Kick Ass Your Life - https://www.forwardthinkingpublishing.com/authors-and-books-2/ann-hobbs/ [Ann Hobbs 2016]

Mental Health - https://www.mayoclinic.org/healthy-lifestyle/adult-health/in-depth/mental-health/art-20044098 [By Mayo Clinic Staff – 2022]

Mental Health Myths and Facts - https://www.mentalhealth.gov/basics/mental-health-myths-facts [2022]

Mental Illness - https://www.mayoclinic.org/diseases-conditions/mental-illness/symptoms-causes/syc-20374968 [2022]

Neurodivergent – What does it Mean? - https://my.clevelandclinic.org/health/symptoms/23154-neurodivergent#:~:text=Neurodivergent%20is%20a%20non-medical%20term,develop%20or%20work%20more%20typically cally [Cleveland Clinic – 2022]

Positive Psychology - https://positivepsychology.com/dbt-dialectical-behavior-therapy/ [Ackerman & Nash 2017]

Psychology Tools - https://www.psychologytools.com/professional/therapies/dialectical-behavior-therapy-dbt/ [2022]

Psychwire - https://psychwire.com/profiles/cv4k3l/marsha-linehan

Self-Care - https://neurodiversity.be/neurodivergent-adults-and-self-care/ [MAI 2022]

Sensory Overload - https://www.healthline.com/health/sensory-overload *[2018]*

Signs of Mental Health - https://www.healthdirect.gov.au/amp/article/signs-mental-health-issue *[2021]*

Social Anxiety Disorder - https://www.psychologytoday.com/us/conditions/social-anxiety-disorder-social-phobia?amp *[2022]*

Social Anxiety Disorder - https://www.nimh.nih.gov/health/publications/social-anxiety-disorder-more-than-just-shyness *[NIH Publication 2022]*

Social Anxiety Disorder - https://www.mayoclinic.org/diseases-conditions/social-anxiety-disorder/symptoms-causes/syc-20353561 *[Mayo Clinic 2022]*

Stress - https://my.clevelandclinic.org/health/articles/11874-stress *[Cleveland Clinic 2022]*

Positive Psychology - https://positivepsychology.com/positive-psychology-interventions/ *[Chowdhray 2019]*

Therapist Aid Worksheets - *https://www.therapistaid.com/therapy-worksheets/dbt/none* [Therapist Aid 2022]

The Neurodivergent Brain - https://www.verywellhealth.com/neurodivergent-5216749 -

[Rudy – 2022]

The Priority Matrix - https://www.planetneurodivergent.com/everyday-coping-techniques-for-neurodivergents/amp/ [2020]

Tips to Manage Depression - https://adaa.org/understanding-anxiety/depression/tips [2022]

Thought Record - https://www.psychologytools.com/self-help/thought-records/ [2022]

What does it mean to be neurodivergent - https://www.verywellmind.com/what-is-neurodivergence-and-what-does-it-mean-to-be-neurodivergent-5196627#:~:text=It%20is%20not%20a%20disability [Ariane Resnick 2022]

What is Neurodiversity? - https://www.webmd.com/add-adhd/features/what-is-neurodiversity [Smitha Bhandari, MD 2021]

NOTES

3. DBT (DIALECTICAL BEHAVIORAL THERAPY)

1. https://psychwire.com/profiles/cv4k3l/marsha-linehan

5. EMOTIONAL REGULATION

1. Feelings Wheel by Geoffrey Roberts

Printed in Great Britain
by Amazon